HOTSPOTS
RHOD

Written by Chris and Melanie Rice, updated by Jane Egginton
Front cover photography courtesy of Thomas Cook Tour Operations Ltd

Original design concept by Studio 183 Limited
Series design by the Bridgewater Book Company
Cover design/artwork by Lee Biggadike, Studio 183 Limited

Produced by the Bridgewater Book Company
The Old Candlemakers, West Street, Lewes, East Sussex BN7 2NZ, United Kingdom
www.bridgewaterbooks.co.uk
Project Editor: Emily Casey Bailey
Project Designer: Lisa McCormick

Published by Thomas Cook Publishing
A division of Thomas Cook Tour Operations Limited
PO Box 227, Units 15-16, Coningsby Road, Peterborough PE3 8SB, United Kingdom
email: books@thomascook.com
www.thomascookpublishing.com
+ 44 (0) 1733 416477

ISBN-13: 978-1-84157-540-7
ISBN-10: 1-84157-540-2

First edition © 2006 Thomas Cook Publishing
Text © 2006 Thomas Cook Publishing
Maps © 2006 Thomas Cook Publishing
Project Editor: Diane Ashmore
Production/DTP Editor: Steven Collins

Printed and bound in Spain by Graficas Cems, Navarra, Spain

CONTENTS

SYMBOLS KEY
The following is a key to the symbols used throughout this book:

i information office	**police station**	**restaurant**
P car park	**airport**	**café**
bus stop	**tip**	**bar**
post office	**shopping**	**fine dining**
church		

---

telephone   **fax**   **email**   **website address**

address   **opening times**   **important**

€ budget price   **€€** mid-range price   **€€€** most expensive

★ special interest   **★★** see if passing   **★★★** top attraction

---

INTRODUCTION
Getting to know Rhodes & Kos

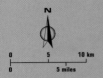

N

0   5   10 km
0   5 miles

KALYMNOS
POTHIA
PSERIMOS
KD
TO
MARMARI   TINGAKI
            ZIA
        PYLI   846 m
MASTICHARI   TOLARI   EDRO
    ANTIMACHIA   THERM
        KOS   KARDAMENA
KARMARI
KEFALOS

AEGEAN SEA

MANDRAKI   PALI
        NISYROS

T

ALBANIA

GREECE   Aegean
            Sea

Ionian   TURKEY
Sea

            KOS

        RHODES

Mediterranean
Sea

BODRUM

TURKEY

MARMARIS

SYMI
YIALOS

PANORMITIS

PARADISI
KREMASTI
TRIANTA
IALYSSOS
IXIA
RHODES TOWN

KALITHEA

Butterfly Valley •
KALITHIES
FALIRAKI

Kamiros •
PSINTHOS

AFANDOU
Epta Piges •
KOLYMBIA

KAMIROS
SKALA

HALKI
ARCHANGELOS

EMPONA

SIANA
1215 m
MASARI

CHARAKI
RHODES

MONOLITHOS

POLONIA
LARDOS
LINDOS

ASKLIPIO
PEFKOS

APOLAKKIA
KIOTARI

GENADI

KATTAVIA
PLIMIRI

• Prassonissi

MEDITERRANEAN SEA

Getting to know Rhodes & Kos

WHERE ARE WE?

Rhodes and Kos form part of the Dodecanese, a group of islands that belong to Greece although geographically they are much closer to Turkey – the Turkish mainland is visible from many of the island beaches. The Greek capital, Athens, on the other hand, is a 14-hour ferry journey away.

CLIMATE

The weather is as good a reason as any for coming to Rhodes and Kos. If you're here in July and August, you can expect temperatures of 30°C (86°F) or higher and you're unlikely to see much in the way of rain (on average one day a month). The ancient Greeks put the wonderful climate down to the intervention of the sun god, Helios, and even today Rhodes holds the sunshine record for Greece (over 300 days a year).

BEACHES

The islands' beaches are some of the safest and cleanest in the European Union. In 2005, no fewer than 35 beaches on Rhodes were awarded the much-coveted Blue Flag for excellence. You can drive to a secluded cove or inlet, take a boat out to one of the islands, or simply soak up the sun on the nearest stretch of soft white sand. The amenities too are second to none, with great opportunities for water sports – everything from windsurfing to pedalo rides.

⬤ *The area averages just one day of rain per month in summer*

NATURAL BEAUTY

In the summer months, Rhodes and Kos are a riot of colour. The avenues of the tourist resorts are lined with palm trees, while extra shade is provided by broad-leafed fig trees, ancient planes, red-blossomed pomegranates, acacias, oaks and cypresses. Village gardens are ablaze with jasmine, honeysuckle, hibiscus and morning glory, while purple bougainvillaea trails from the whitewashed houses. The hillsides are planted with vines and, down in the valleys, you'll see orchards bearing a rich harvest of oranges, lemons, olives and figs.

THE PEOPLE

Greek people are extremely friendly and engaging and visitors will quickly be won over by their consideration and courtesy, their ability to relax in the company of strangers, their willingness to share experiences and not least by their excellent command of English.

CHURCHES

The walls and ceilings of Greek churches are covered with vividly painted, but rather sombre, images of Christ and his saints and scenes from the Bible. The main feature of every Orthodox church, however, is the *iconostasis*, a wooden screen, gilded and filled with several tiers of sacred images, which separates the main body of the church from the sanctuary. Only ordained priests are allowed beyond this screen.

If you want to hear a traditional Greek liturgy (the ceremonies have remained largely unchanged for centuries), mass is held in churches all over the island during the week at 19.00. The main Sunday service usually starts at 10.00. Dress respectfully (cover bare shoulders and wear trousers, not shorts).

HISTORY EVERYWHERE

The story of these beautiful islands reaches back into the mists of time, to Homer's *Iliad* and the Trojan Wars. There are reminders of ancient Greek civilization everywhere – perhaps the most evocative are the ruined Acropolis at Lindos and the Asklepion in Kos. The Medieval Rhodes Old Town, complete with castle, has a magical atmosphere and is dotted with interesting historic buildings – some of which have been turned into museums.

THE COLOSSUS

One of Seven Wonders of the Ancient World, the Colossus of Rhodes was a 33 m (over 100 ft) bronze statue, comparable in size to the Statue of Liberty in New York City's harbour. The statue was a monument to the sun god Apollo (Helios in Greek). It took 12 years to construct and was completed around 290 BC. It collapsed around 227 BC following an earthquake and the remains were eventually sold as scrap. Tradition has it that the Colossus straddled Rhodes harbour, but modern archaeologists consider a site slightly inland more likely.

KNIGHTS OF ST JOHN

The religious Order of the Knights of St John was founded in Jerusalem in the 11th century; its members were also known as Hospitallers because of their charitable work with the sick. The Crusades transformed them into a formidable strike force with a mission to expel the Muslims from the Holy Land. In 1248 they moved their headquarters to Rhodes and built some of the greatest medieval fortresses in the world, the remains of which can be seen on 30 spectacular headland sites commanding magnificent coastal views.

SIESTA

The siesta is taken seriously in Greece, and with good reason: it's hot! It begins after lunch at around 14.00 and continues until around 17.00 hours; most shops (and many businesses) close during that period. Everything springs back to life in the early evening and many people continue working until their evening meal at around 21.00 hours.

The best of Rhodes & Kos

REMINDERS OF THE PAST

- See the working windmill at Antimachia, Kos (see page 75).
- Visit one of the local folklore museums, such as the one in Yialos, the capital of the island of Symi (see page 93).
- Tour the castle walls of Rhodes Old Town (see page 14).
- Admire the spectacularly sited fortress of Monolithos on Rhodes and the sheer drop of 235 m (770 ft) to the sea below (see page 34).
- Climb to the Acropolis at Lindos on Rhodes (see page 49).
- Visit the shrine of the healing god Asklepios in Kos (see page 61).

● *The remains of the ancient market or agora in Kos Town*

NATURAL SIGHTS

- Take a boat to the island of Nisyros near Kos (see page 88) and see steam rise from the crater of the volcano or watch for bubbles of volcanic gas in the sea near Kefalos (see page 78).
- Take a walk through Butterfly Valley, near Kremasti, on Rhodes, and admire the rare and colourful Kalimorfa butterfly (see page 33).
- Follow one of the nature trails in the Plaka Forest, Kos (see page 75).

BEST PLACES TO WATCH THE SUNSET

- From a taverna in the mountain village of Zia, Kos (see page 66).
- Gazing across the Aegean from the ruins of the ancient city of Kamiros, Rhodes (see page 34).
- From the arms of the cross at Filerimos, Rhodes (see page 28).
- Watch the dying rays light up the north-western coastline of Kos from the terrace of one of the best fish restaurants on the island – the Limionas Fish Taverna (see page 79).

EXCURSIONS

- Spice up your stay in Rhodes or Kos by doing a little bit of island hopping. As you'll soon discover, each island is different – although happily they all have more than their fair share of sun, sea and sand. This is also one of the best ways to experience the traditional Greek way of life at first hand.
- You can sample a different culture entirely by taking a day excursion to Turkey. It is best to arrange the trip through your holiday representative to avoid any visa irregularities.

RESORTS
Rhodes

Rhodes Town
City of the Rose

In its 2400-year history, the 'City of the Rose' has seen them all: Greeks, Romans, Byzantines, Crusader Knights, Turks, Italians and, latterly, tourists. Modern Rhodes Town, with a population of around 65,000, offers a range of historical sights as well as excellent shopping, a pulsating nightlife and a good selection of places to eat. What's more, it is the perfect base for exploring the whole island.

Rhodes Town presents a dual face – the **Old Town** and the **New Town**. The modern island capital, centred on **Mandraki Harbour**, is a cosmopolitan district of tree-lined boulevards, imposing public buildings, luxury hotels, international restaurants, intense nightlife and a dazzling array of shops. You'll also find here the casino, municipal art gallery and beaches.

Exploring the sights and monuments of the Old Town is a must. Preserved as a Unesco World Heritage Site, it is the world's best example of a medieval walled town. The moat between the inner and outer walls has never contained water, but was simply a device to prevent invaders from employing siege towers. Today, the Old Town is a fascinating mix of cobbled streets, squares and courtyards, churches, mosques and massive fortifications – all dominated by the **Palace of the Grand Masters**.

The Old Town has two main areas: the Bourg (including the ancient Turkish quarter, bazaar and the old Jewish enclave) and the Knights' Quarter. Be sure to walk down **Odos Ippoton (Knights' Street),** where the Orders' seven nations built their beautiful Gothic Inns or headquarters. The Inn of France is the largest and most impressive, with its magnificent crocodile gargoyles. The Inn of England is on **Moussion Square**. It was abandoned in 1534, when Henry VIII was excommunicated by the Pope.

The Knights were carers as well as soldiers. You can visit their Hospital, also on Moussion Square, where one of the original wards has been preserved. The building also contains an impressive Archaeological Museum, reflecting the island's prestigious history. Practically next door is the Decorative Arts Collection, with some exquisite artefacts.

⬢ *Rhodes Old Town is a fine example of a medieval walled town*

The highest viewpoint in town is the Byzantine clock tower at the top of Sokratous Street in the Old Town. On a clear day it affords dazzling views of the entire island and the Turkish coast. 🕐 Open 09.00–late ⓘ Admission charge includes a drink in the café half-way up

THINGS TO SEE & DO
Mandraki Harbour ★★

Rhodes' harbour was once the site of the ancient 30.5 m (100 ft) tall Colossus of Rhodes, one of the Seven Wonders of the Ancient World. Nowadays, it is full of excursion boats, pleasure cruisers and luxury yachts from all over the world. Its entrance is guarded by bronze statues of a stag and a doe, the island's mascots. The three medieval windmills on its eastern breakwater were built to mill grain for the departing cargo

boats (one has been restored to working order) and, just beyond, the
Fort of Saint Nicholas contains a lighthouse and chapel dedicated
to the patron saint of sailors. The harbour is lined with colourful cafés –
great for a cold beer or a cocktail.

Palace of the Grand Masters ★★★

This formidable citadel was constructed by the Knights of St John in
the 14th century and restored for Mussolini, the Italian dictator, as a
summer residence. Of the 158 rooms, about 24 are open to the public.
The marble floors are decorated with exquisite mosaics (Roman in
origin) of dolphins, sea-horses, tigers, gladiators and mythical beasts.
🕘 Open Tues–Sun 08.30–15.00 ❶ Admission charge, guided tours

Odos Ippoton (Street of the Knights) ★★

Leading east from the Palace, this is said to be the oldest street in
Greece. Following a 5th-century-BC layout, it is lined with fine medieval
'inns', which once housed the Knights of St John.

Rodini Park ★

Cool, shady and peaceful, this beautifully landscaped park is the perfect
antidote to a morning's sightseeing in the Old Town. It is densely
wooded, and the air carries the scent of cypress, pine and oleander.
Take any of the paths and you'll soon be within earshot of the gurgling
stream, although keep an eye on very young children as the paths are
unfenced and may have a steep drop either side. There's also a children's

---

Guided tours of the walls and fortifications of **Rhodes Castle**,
a masterpiece of medieval engineering, take place on Tuesday and
Saturday afternoons. Wear comfortable, non-slip shoes with good ankle
support: the fallen stones are unstable and can make walking difficult.
Parents should take particular care with young children as there are no
guard rails inside the castle. Meet in front of the Palace of the Grand
Masters at 14.45.

---

playground. ❶ Take the no. 3 bus from the harbour, or it's a 3 km (1¾ mile) walk along Lindou

Scuba diving ★

An unforgettable experience. One- and four-day courses are available, and boats leave from the harbour for Kalithea Bay (near Faliraki) where the crystal-clear waters are perfect for observing the marine life. You get a chance to feed the fish and you'll be photographed underwater as a memento of the adventure. Equipment is provided and the instruction is by qualified and experienced PADI divers. Ask your holiday representative for more details.

Sokratous Street ★★

Colourful Sokratous Street is the street bazaar of the Old Town. Here you can buy everything from leather bags and jewellery to CDs and cuddly toys. Half-way down, at no. 17, is a typical *kafeneion*, or coffee shop, dating back to Ottoman times – note the pebbled floor and the men playing backgammon. The faded red building at the top of Sokratous is the Mosque of Suleyman, founded in the 16th century to commemorate the Turkish conquest of Rhodes.

Sound and Light Show ★★

A dramatic re-creation of the siege of Rhodes by the Turks in 1522, culminating in the last-ditch stand taken by the Knights against Suleiman the Magnificent (not suitable for very young children). English language narration nightly except Sunday.

BEACHES

Elli Beach (20 minutes' walk from Mandraki Harbour, on the tip of the Island) is the most popular beach in Rhodes. Sheltered from the wind, it has a diving platform as well as sunbeds, umbrellas and refreshment facilities. The breezy **Akti Kanari Beach** is more suitable for activities and water sports.

0

300 m

0

300 yds

MEDITERRANEAN SEA

FORT OF
SAINT NICHOLAS

Mandraki
Harbour

GOVERNMENT
HOUSE

11

25 MARTIOU

APOL

AMER

7

12

9

IROON POLYTECHNICOU

Elli Beach

3

AQUARIUM

G. PAPANIKOLAOU

DRAGOUMI IONOS

28 OKTOVRIOU

ALEX D

S

Akti Kanari
'Windy' Beach

MANDILARA

ORFANIDOU

AKTI MIAOULI

13

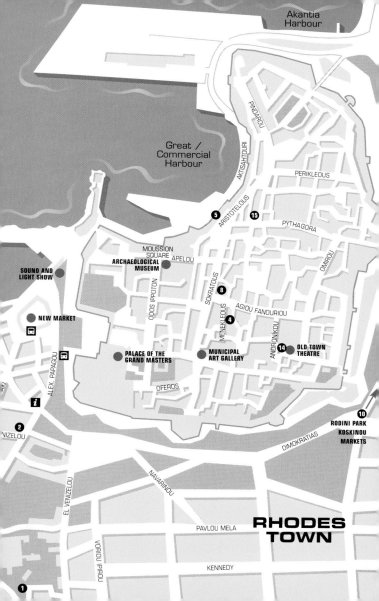

Akantia
Harbour

Great /
Commercial
Harbour

PINDAROU

AKTISAHTOURI

PERIKLEOUS

5 **15**

ARISTOTELOUS

PYTHAGORA

OMIROU

MOUSSION
SQUARE

APELOU

**ARCHAEOLOGICAL
MUSEUM**

SOKRATOUS

8

AGIOU FANOURIOU

ODOS IPITON

MENEKLEOUS

4

**SOUND AND
LIGHT SHOW**

NEW MARKET

**PALACE OF THE
GRAND MASTERS**

**MUNICIPAL
ART GALLERY**

ANDRONIKOU

14 **OLD TOWN
THEATRE**

ALEX. PAPAGOU

OFEROS

i

2

NIZELOU

10

**RODINI PARK
KOSKINOU
MARKETS**

DIMOKRATIAS

EL VENIZELOU

NAVARINOU

VGRIOU IPIROU

PAVLOU MELA

RHODES
TOWN

KENNEDY

1

RESTAURANTS & BARS (see map on pages 18–19)

Capricci €€ ❶ This restaurant provides a high standard of cuisine and service, with a pleasant decor. Try their freshly cooked Italian food, with a choice of 16 different homemade pizzas, and enjoy stunning seaviews at sunset. ⓐ 17 Akti Kanari ❶ 22410 33395 🕐 Open 19.30–late

El Divino € ❷ This elegant, Italian-style café-bar is currently *the* place to see and be seen in town. ⓐ 5 Alex. Diakou ❶ 22410 39041 🕐 Open 08.30–01.00 (Jun–Oct)

Ellinikon €€€ ❸ Romantic atmosphere, outdoor garden and excellent Greek cuisine, just across from Casino Rodos. ⓐ 6 Papanikolaou ❶ 22410 28111 🕐 Open 19.00–01.00

Fotis €€€ ❹ A seafood *taverna* with excellent cuisine, great service and a delightful atmosphere. A favourite choice of the local residents – always a good sign. Indoor and outdoor seating is available. ⓐ 8 Menekleous, Old Town ❶ 22410 27359 ⓦ www.fotisgroup.com 🕐 Open 08.30–01.00

Four Seasons €€€ ❺ Restaurant located in the Old Town serving Mediterranean dishes, meat and seafood entrées. Cosy décor ⓐ 38 Aristotelous ❶ 22410 70523 🕐 Open 13.00–16.00 and 19.00–midnight

McDonalds € ❻ Right in the centre of Rhodes, in a Baroque Italian-style house. Small play area for children. Will deliver to your apartment or hotel! ⓐ 50 Gr. Lambraki ❶ 22410 70777 🕐 Open Sun–Thurs 09.00–01.00 and Fri–Sat 09.00–02.00

Rodon Café €€€ ❼ For a more sophisticated palate, serving intercontinental cuisine, choice meats, fresh fish and delectable desserts. Great for a special evening out, with live music and dancing every night. See the decorative photos outlining the history of the oldest hotel in Rhodes from 1938 to the present day. ⓐ Casino Rodos, 4 Papanikolaou ⓣ 22410 97500 ⓛ Open 20.00–02.00

Romeo €€ ❽ Good-value, authentic Greek cuisine in an ancient setting at the heart of the Old Town, with live bouzouki music every evening. ⓐ 7–9 Menekleous, Old Town ⓣ 22410 25186 ⓛ Open 10.00–midnight

Swedco Bakery € ❾ This establishment offers an excellent breakfast or brunch, freshly cooked gourmet food, and delightful decor with bottles of wine and jars of homemade marmalade lining the walls. Did we forget to mention the delicious Swedish pastries? ⓐ 4 Iroon Polytechnicou ⓣ 22410 35660 ⓛ Open 04.00–22.00

Yiannis Koskinou €€ ❿ Do not miss eating here in the small village of Koskinou, with its narrow streets and white-washed houses. This is one of the best home-style Greek restaurants. Try their wine from Alexandris in Embona. Best to go before 21.00 as there may well be a wait of about 10–15 minutes later in the evening, especially in high season. ⓐ Koskinou ⓣ 22410 63547 ⓛ Open 18.00–midnight

NIGHTLIFE

At the last count there were more than 600 bars in Rhodes, mostly concentrated in the New Town. Orfanidou is the official 'Bar Street' but Diakou doesn't lag far behind.

Blue Lagoon ⓫ This has to seen to be believed. Inside is a ship, a lake, a haunted house (ⓛ Open 19.00–23.30)and waiters dressed as pirates. It's great for children in the daytime, and wild by night too. In the same entertainment centre the **Studio Gas Dance Station** plays dance music till dawn, and the owner has just opened the nearby **le Palias Café**. All three venues: ⓐ 2, 25 Martiou ⓣ 22410 32632/76072 ⓛ Open 09.00–04.00

Casino Rodos ⓬ A casino with two restaurants and changing shows. Minimum age to enter gaming area is 23 years so remember to bring your passport. ⓐ 4 Papanikolaou ⓣ 22410 97500 ⓦ www.casinorodos.gr ⓛ Open Mon–Thurs 15.00–06.00 and Fri 14.00 through to Mon 06.00 ⓘ Admission charge (valid for 24 hours and includes free drinks)

Colorado ⓭ One of Bar Street's liveliest venues, which includes a live rock club and several discos. ⓐ 57 Orfanidou ⓣ 22410 75120 ⓦ www.coloradoclub.gr ⓛ Rock club open 20.00–06.00

🔽 *Rhodes Old Town and harbour*

Folk Dance Theatre ⑭ Experience local folk tradition at first hand with live Greek dance performances in traditional costumes.
📍 Old Town Theatre, off Andronikou 📞 22410 2015
🕑 Performances Mon, Wed and Fri 21.20

Havana ⑮ Great music and atmosphere, located in the Old Town's Bar Street. Castle-like rooms lit by candlelight. 📍 Miltiadi Street, Old Town
📞 6932 278587 🕑 Open 21.00–03.00

SHOPPING

The main shopping areas are around Plateia Kipriou in the New Town (you'll find **Marks & Spencer** and **Bhs** here, as well as numerous boutiques), and Sokratous Street in the Old Town. Try **Byzantine Icons** (📍 81 Sokratous Street) filled from top to bottom with Greek icons; **Marinos Wine** offering over 500 labels of wine, plus spirits, beers and champagne, at amazingly low prices (📍 23–25 28 October Street); **Blacksmith** (📍 119 Sokratous Street) for toys and gifts made from olive wood; **The Green Shop** (📍 162–164 Sokratous Street) for herbs, spices, honeys, mountain teas and oils; **Freshline Soaps** (📍 13 Ammochostou Street) for aromatic soaps, lotions, and baby products which contain environmentally friendly Greek ingredients. **The Ministry of Culture museum shop** has reproductions of ancient artefacts, such as statues and vases. Most shops in the Old Town stay open until 22.30.

Markets

The largest **fruit and vegetable market** in the Dodecanese is held on Zefiros Street (next to the cemetery) every Wednesday and Saturday; there's a similar market on Vironas Street (near the Stadium) every Thursday. The **Nea Agora** ('New Market') beside Mandraki Harbour has a handful of daily stalls selling fruit and vegetables.

Ixia
excellent base for water sports

Just a five-minute drive from the amenities of Rhodes Town, Ixia (pronounced 'Ix-ear') is one of the most fashionable beach resorts on the island. Take a gentle stroll along the main street, Ialyssos Avenue (pronounced 'ee-ala-sos'), and you'll quickly become familiar with all that's available here, from the star-rated facilities of the luxury hotels to the neon-lit bars and restaurants catering to all ages and tastes. The long stretch of beach is never more than 50 m (55 yds) away, the sea is turquoise and translucent and there are views across to the mountains of Turkey.

Onshore breezes generate the waves that make Ixia absolutely ideal for windsurfing. Surfboards and pedalos can be hired from stalls in front of the Rodos Hilton and Olympic Palace hotels. Swimming in the choppy seas is exhilarating for adults but young children may prefer the hotel pool. There's plenty of elbow room at Ixia but if you want more privacy try one of the coves near **Psaropoula** (between Monte Smith and Rhodes Town). There is also a kilometre-long walkway along the coves near **Psaraoula**. It's great for an evening stroll, looking at the beautiful rock formations.

For a romantic evening walk it's difficult to beat **Monte Smith** with its unsurpassed views over Ixia and across to the Turkish coast. The Mini Train Trolley offers a 45-minute tour of the outskirts of the Old Town and up towards Monte Smith. Only a short walk from the ancient acropolis of Rhodes, you can also get there by bus no. 5 from Mandraki. Monte Smith is named after Sir Sydney Smith, the British Admiral who observed the manoeuvres of Napoleon's Egyptian fleet from here in 1802.

◀ *There's plenty of room on Ixia's beach*

THINGS TO SEE & DO
Coastal walk ★★
Take a walk along a footpath which runs from Isia bay into Rhodes town for a bit of exercise and great views.

Mini-golf ★
Try your hand at the 18-hole mini-golf in the cool, shaded gardens in front of the Olympic Palace Hotel. ⓐ Ialyssos Avenue ❶ 22410 39790 🕐 Open 10.00–23.00

RESTAURANTS & BARS

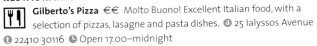

🍴 **Gilberto's Pizza** €€ Molto Buono! Excellent Italian food, with a selection of pizzas, lasagne and pasta dishes. ⓐ 25 Ialyssos Avenue ❶ 22410 30116 🕐 Open 17.00–midnight

🍴 **Golden Wheat** €€ Enjoy succulent Chinese dishes in this pleasant air-conditioned restaurant. Set meals for two and four. ⓐ 143 Ialyssos Avenue ❶ 22410 96159 🕐 Open 17.00–01.00

🍴 **Napoli** €€ A friendly restaurant serving a wide range of pastas and pizzas, plus tasty traditional Greek dishes. ⓐ Ialyssos Avenue (near Hippocampus) ❶ 22410 90119 🕐 Open noon–midnight

🍸 **Phillip's Bar** € The oldest bar in town attracts an older clientele. Many devotees return year after year to enjoy Phillip's hospitality. Overlooking the rooftops of Ixia, the roof-garden serves full English breakfasts, sausages and mash, and mugs of Nescafé by day, English beers and cocktails by night. ⓐ 18 Venizelou ❶ 22410 90366 🕐 Open 08.30–02.00

🍴 **Poseidonia** €€ Smart Greek restaurant with garden terrace. Also karaoke nights. ⓐ 9 Iraklidon ❶ 22410 22276 🕐 Open 09.00–22.30

SHOPPING

All the shops are on the main street, Iraklidon/Ialyssos Avenue. As well as a supermarket (**Pappou**) and bakery, you will find the jewellers **Gold Effie** and **Antoniadi Gold Bazaar**, the leather shop **Emmanuel Zannis**, and **Periklis** which sells hand-painted plates, jugs and other hand-crafted souvenirs.

Sofitel Capsis Hotel €€ There are three restaurants in this luxury hotel, so take your pick. International and local dishes at Pandora. ⓐ Ialyssos Avenue ⓣ 22410 25015 ⓛ Open 11.00–late

Stani by the Pool € Best homemade ice cream on the island! This is a great place to take children for amazing ice cream creations served in large decorative dessert dishes. There is also a large tranquil pool and a playground to keep children entertained. ⓐ Iraklidon (across from Avra Beach Hotel) within a mini shopping mall ⓣ 22410 91422 ⓛ Open 07.00–01.00

NIGHTLIFE

Sofitel Capsis Hotel This five-star hotel has four bars, including a cocktail bar. ⓐ Ialyssos Avenue ⓣ 22410 25015 ⓛ Open 11.00–late

⬤ *A typical snack menu*

● The beach at Trianta is pebble and sand

Trianta
traditional Greek atmosphere

The name Trianta (pronounced 'Tri-anda' and sometimes spelt 'Trianda')
comes from the Greek word for '30' and refers to the 30 stone houses
which were built here by the Knights of St John in the Middle Ages.
This traditional Greek village on the Filerimos road rubs along nicely
with its modern counterpart, only 500 m (550 yds) from the beach.
Here you'll find all the usual tourist amenities from supermarkets
and souvenir shops to family-friendly restaurants, bars, and even
a nightclub. There are regular buses to Ixia and Rhodes Town, while
taxis are cheap and plentiful.

Just a short, picturesque drive from Trianta is the restored hilltop
monastery of **Filerimos**, built by the Knights of St John (Medieval period)
on the ruins of ancient Ialyssos. The remnants of a Greek temple, the
cross-shaped baptistry of the first Christian basilica, and the tiny
underground chapel of St George, with 15th-century wall paintings,
can all be seen in front of the steps that lead to the monastery. Roman
Catholic as well as Greek Orthodox Christians worshipped the icon of

the Virgin of Filerimos, in the hexagonal Church of the Knights, though at separate altars. To the rear of the monastery are the impressive remains of the Byzantine garrison. As a souvenir of your visit, try *sette erbe* ('seven herbs'), a green liqueur produced by the monks. ● Open Tues–Fri 08.00–20.00, Sat–Mon 08.30–15.00 ● Dress modestly

Running at right angles to the monastery is a tree-lined avenue known as **Golgotha**. At the far end of the path is a 14.6 m (48 ft) high cross which visitors can climb for breathtaking views of the island – even more so at sunset.

THINGS TO SEE & DO
Children's activities ★
Luna Park miniature go-kart circuit Suitable for accompanied children up to the age of about ten. Buggies and motor bikes (including three- and four-wheeled bikes) all with seat belts. ⓐ In Trianta ● Open 10.00–22.00

Planet Z An indoor playground and café suitable for younger children. It is air-conditioned and safe, as the play area is enclosed and has floor padding and safety nets. Toys are also sold. ⓐ Ialyssos Beach Road ⓘ 22410 94428 ● Open 19.00–21.30

Cycle hire ★
Mountain bikes are available for hire by the day and can be used for doing the shopping, getting you to and from the beach, or exploring nearby villages and resorts (Ixia and Kremasti for example). Energetic cyclists might consider making the trip to Filerimos on two wheels (5 km/3 miles, but a tough climb). **Ideal MTB Rental** ⓐ 3 Iraklidon, Trianta ⓣ 22410 92872 (mobile: 6946 572126) ● Open 08.30–20.30

Mike's Horse Riding ★
A tiny stables on the road to Filerimos offers lessons and short treks for riders of all ages and standards. ⓐ On the road to Filerimos ⓘ 22410 94277 ● Open 10.00–13.30 and 15.30–19.30

Sport ★

On the road from Trianta to Kremasti, **Adonis Energy Club** offers aerobics and weight training, sauna, basketball, beach volleyball, table tennis, junior aerobics and light refreshments. ☎ 22410 94786 ⏰ Open Mon–Fri 09.00–22.00, Sat 10.00–21.00

Windsurfing ★

The bay is ideal for windsurfing. **The Oxbow Club** stocks equipment, repairs sails and offers lessons. ⓐ 1 Ferinikis Street ☎ 22410 91666 ⏰ Open noon–20.00

 For a taste of traditional Greek entertainment, there is live bouzouki music most nights in the main square (by the Café Royal).

BEACHES

The pebble-and-sand beach at Trianta is suitable for swimming, but the water can be choppy and there's a strong current – young children should stay within the roped-off areas or swim in the hotel pools. Pedalos and windsurfing equipment can be hired at the beach. There are more comprehensive water sports facilities at nearby Ixia (page 25).

SHOPPING

 The main shopping street is Ferinikis. For leather goods, jewellery, clothing and gifts, check out **Pazoyros**, **Theresa Silver**, **Coral Reef** and **Leena's Shop**.

Zum Zum supermarket Newspapers, alcohol and groceries.
ⓐ Opposite the Blue Horizon hotel, 15 Ferinikis

Emmanuel This is a tourist shop/supermarket. ⓐ 1 Ierou Lohou
⏰ Open 07.00–midnight

Va Gelis Sells smart leather purses and handbags and gypsum ornaments, jewellery and novelties. ⓐ 19 Ierou Lohou

Fuji Film Photo Shop Have your snapshots printed. ⓐ Ferinikis

RESTAURANTS & BARS

 Bora Kai €€ Polynesian dishes supplement the Chinese cuisine here, where the menu features exotic names, like sea-treasure curry, Mongolian beef and Fiji duck. ⓐ Ferinikis Street, opposite the Blue Horizon Hotel ❶ 22410 94328 ❶ Open 18.00–midnight

 Café Hellas € This smart, typically Greek café (part of the Forum Hotel), with a shady terrace, is a good spot for afternoon tea. ⓐ Ferinikis Street ❶ 22410 94321 ❶ Open 09.00–midnight

 **Debby's** € This friendly snack bar is popular with English visitors and has a loyal clientele. Breakfast is available most of the day and there's a range of evening meals. Satellite TV. ⓐ 41 Ialyssos Avenue, opposite the Maribel Apartments ❶ 22410 93600 ❶ Open 09.00–late

 Kioupia €€ This restaurant has a fixed price menu, so don't worry about not knowing what to order. They'll serve a variety of fantastic dishes at a set price. ⓐ 12 Treis ❶ Open 19.30–01.00

Sports Bar Nirvana € Enjoy a cocktail or beer and see world sports on a life-sized satellite TV. ⓐ Ferinikis Street ❶ Open 09.00–03.00

Windmill Restaurant €€ Have a lunch or dinner on the deck overlooking picturesque Ialyssos beach. Greek and international cuisine. ⓐ Ialyssos Beach ❶ Open 09.00–late

NIGHTLIFE

BO Club A new club on the main road, popular with the young set, and playing a wide mixture of music including hits from the 1970s and 1980s, house, disco and underground. ⓐ 2 Iraklidon ❶ Bar open 21.00– midnight ❶ Disco open 23.30–05.00 ❶ Free entrance until 00.30

Ne 1! Bar serving cocktails. ⓐ Ferinikis Street ❶ 22410 90084 ❶ Open 21.00–04.00

Kremasti
peaceful and picturesque

In small, friendly Kremasti (pronounced 'Kre-masti') holidaymakers mingle happily with locals in the shops and cafés on the main village street. A world away from the commercialization of the larger resorts, Kremasti is handy for exploring the picturesque mountain villages of the interior, yet just a short bus ride from the sights and nightclubs of Rhodes Town.

A stroll through Kremasti village reveals many hidden surprises. Most visitors will be familiar with the gleaming white tower of the **parish church** (a local landmark), but take a look inside. The walls are covered with delicately painted frescoes, showing scenes from the Bible and the lives of the saints, while the gilded frame of the *iconostasis* – the altar screen which is a feature of all Orthodox churches – is illuminated by flickering candlelight, creating an atmosphere of awe and reverence.

As you leave the church you'll see the men of the village congregating outside the local library. They come here to chat over a glass of coffee, to play backgammon or just to watch the world go by. Take any side turning from the main road and you'll come across traditional flat-roofed houses. Take a closer look at the courtyards where, under the lemon trees, families do their washing and cooking and even bed down under the stars on hot summer nights.

● *Picturesque Kremasti*

THINGS TO SEE & DO
Strike Bowling Alley ⋆

Wind down in the evening with a game of bowling at the 8-lane bowling alley. Air-conditioned, serving cheap eats, coffees, cocktails and ice cream. Also has computers with internet access, a pool table and video games.

ⓐ Eleftherias Avenue ⓘ 22410 93229 ⓛ Open 10.00–02.00

 While exploring south-west Rhodes, stop for lunch at one of the quayside seafood restaurants in Kamiros Skala, or try **Johnny's Fish Taverna** just beyond, overlooking a sheltered cove and tiny pebbled beach.

EXCURSIONS
Butterfly Valley ⋆⋆

A short drive inland will take you to **Petaloudes**, a scenic gorge which, from May to September, is home to the rare and eye-catching Jersey Tiger moths. These delicate creatures appear well camouflaged when their wings are folded, but are red in flight. There are shady walks through the woods and a restaurant with tables overlooking a waterfall and bubbling stream. If you're feeling energetic, a trail leads uphill to the 18th-century monastery of **Panagia Kalopetra** (ⓘ 22440 81801 ⓛ Open 08.30–sunset ⓘ Admission charge), where there are wonderful views and picnic tables.

Ostrich Farm ⋆

Visit the ostriches and other animals at this modest-sized farm. For a unique experience try the ostrich burgers in the restaurant, but for those less daring there are also local dishes. Souvenir shop and playground for children on site. ⓐ On the road to Butterfly Valley ⓘ (mobile) 6945 327142 ⓛ Open 09.00–sunset ⓘ Admission fee, but free for children under 3 years

Scenic drive ⋆⋆⋆

Kremasti makes the ideal starting point for a tour of Rhodes' south-west coast. Take the coastal road past the airport and continue through the villages of **Paradissi, Theologos** and **Soroni**, until you reach **Kamiros**. Set inland amidst pine trees, the site of ancient **Kamiros** is one of the three ancient settlements on Rhodes, and one of the best-preserved classical towns in Greece (🕐 Open Tues–Sun 08.00–18.40, last entrance 20 minutes before closing ❶ Admission charge).

Follow the coastal road to the fishing village of **Kamiros Skala** and then turn inland into the rugged mountains, with glimpses of the Knights' 16th-century hillside fortress to the right. Picturesque **Kritinia** is worth a stop, before continuing on to **Siana**, a delightful village where time stands still – the hands on the church clock are painted on. Shop here for thyme honey and souma (a local liquor), before heading on to **Monolithos**. This village takes its name from the 250 m (820 ft) high rock (mono meaning 'one', lithos meaning 'rock') just beyond the village, with an ancient castle perched precariously at its summit. From here, the road snakes down to a small, rocky beach, a pleasant stop for a dip in the sea.

Head back to Kremasti via **Empona**, noted for wine and folk dancing. Visit **Emery wine factory** on the outskirts of the village for visits and tastings (🕐 Open 09.00–16.30), and **Alexandris Wines**, which is located in the basement of a house. Ask a local for directions!

BEACHES

Kremasti beach, with views across to Turkey, is just seven minutes' walk from the village centre. Loungers and umbrellas are available for hire and there are showers and café facilities.

RESTAURANTS & BARS

 Bee Garden €€ Chinese and Korean fare. Suitable for a special night out. ⓐ 26 Kremasti Avenue (opposite Filerimos Apartments) ☎ 22410 94970 🕐 Open 19.00–midnight

 Grande Classic Café € Café-lounge offering Greek cuisine for breakfast, lunch or dinner. Lively atmosphere and pleasant decor. ⓐ 53 Eleftherias 🕐 Open 08.00–05.00

Masasoura €€€ A must if you visit Maritsa: excellent Greek cuisine. Outdoor dining is available ⓐ Platia Maritsown Maritsa. ⓣ 22410 48109 ⓛ Open all year Mon–Sun 20.00–midnight

 Melba's Kitchen € Pasta dishes and local specialities on a fast-food menu ⓐ 59 Eleftherias ⓕ 22410 91004 ⓛ Open 11.00–16.00 and 18.00–midnight

Odyssey € Enjoy a romantic drink in the attractive garden of this café-bar ⓐ Eleftherias ⓣ 22410 9171 ⓛ Open 10.00–02.30

The Village Inn €€ A typical English pub. Terrace, salad bar, patio and beer garden ⓐ Niridon Street (the road to the beach) ⓣ 22410 95045 ⓛ Open noon–03.00

NIGHTLIFE

Melody Palace Smart club with live bouzouki music, and traditional dancing. ⓐ Eleftherias ⓛ Open 23.00–05.00

Steps Rooftop Bar Great place for couples wanting a cocktail, nice garden atmosphere. International music until midnight. ⓐ Eleftherias ⓛ Open until midnight

SHOPPING

Apart from the supermarket in Neriethon Road, most shops are on the High Street. **Foto Helios** has a 20-minute film-developing service. **Karelia** stocks English paperbacks and newspapers. **Scarpomania** sells leather bags, shoes, belts and canvas bags. The **Kremasti Fair**, renowned throughout the island, takes place between 8 and 15 August with craft and food stalls, music and dancing.

Faliraki
the party resort

Faliraki (pronounced 'Faly-raki') prides itself on being the island's 'party resort' and the nightlife is certainly a major source of appeal. The beach is its other trump card – 5 km (3 miles) of golden sand offering every amenity for action seekers, including a full range of water sports.

There are lots of restaurants, bars and nightclubs in Faliraki, all within a 20-minute walk from the beach. **Ermou** is 'Bar Street' but the pavements of **Kalithea Avenue** also resound to the disco beat after sundown. Many bars remain open well after midnight.

Faliraki boasts one of the Irish bars, **Kelly's**, on Rhodes, and one of the few genuine Scottish bars in the Aegean – at **The Tartan Arms** the waiters even wear kilts! There are karaoke bars, cocktail bars, sports bars and bars with giant TV screens showing movies or Sky sports. The clubs cater for all musical tastes – 1960s' nostalgia, garage, house and techno. Many are hosted by British DJs and there are theme evenings and laser shows.

Following several incidents of drunken loutish behaviour amongst partying tourists, the Greek authorities have come down hard on offenders. It is wise to be cautious when out on the town, and not do anything that might be deemed offensive or illegal.

THINGS TO SEE & DO
Go-karting ★
The small racetrack here is ideal for children. ● Between the Rhodes–Lindos road and Kalithea Avenue opposite the funfair ● 22410 86151 ● Open 14.00–23.00

Golf ★
George's Crazy Golf (● just off the main Rhodes–Lindos road ● 22410 85596 ● Open 08.00–01.00) and **Kresten Palace** (on Kalithea Avenue ● 22410 62714 ● Open 10.00–midnight) has an 18-hole course nearby, and minigolf and tennis in its grounds.

H2O ★

Relax by the pool or check out the disco. A snack bar is available during the day. Fri and Sat bazouki music and live entertainment. ➌ Kalithea Falirakiou Street ➊ 22410 87801 ⏰ Open 24 hours; snack bar closes 23.00; disco opens 23.00

Water Park ★★

Five different water slides, a wave pool, aqua gym, pirate ship and water guns. For the more adventurous, there are the Kamikaze and Free Fall rides. Food is available. Free bus from Mandraki harbour. ➋ On Faliraki's coastal road ➊ 22410 84303 🌐 www.water-park.gr/ ⏰ Open 09.30–18.00; open until 19.00 (June, July and August)

Water sports and outdoor activities ★★

Gabriel's and Theo's (on Faliraki beach) between them offer water-skiing, paragliding, catamaran sailing (lessons available), snorkelling, and pedalo hire. Or take your life in your hands and go bungee jumping with **New World Bungee** (the crane is a local landmark). Just behind the beach is the **Slingshot** – strap yourself in and enjoy being 'blasted into space' at a rate of 0 to 160 km/h (0 to 100 mph) in less than three seconds. There's also 'sky surfing', combining the sensation of hang-gliding with the exhilaration of skydiving from a height of 45 m (150 ft).

ANTHONY QUINN

The Oscar-winning star of American movies Anthony Quinn shaped the popular image of Greece in no small degree when he played the title role in the film *Zorba the Greek* – remember Zorba's dance and the infectious music of Mikis Theodorakis? Quinn fell in love with Rhodes while filming *The Guns of Navarone* on the island in 1961 – several scenes were shot at what is now known as Anthony Quinn Bay, near Faliraki.

BEACHES

All the beaches mentioned here have been given the coveted Blue Flag award. **Faliraki Bay** is gently shelving and is ideal for young children. Some 4 km (2½ miles) north is **Kalithea**, a thermal spa valued since ancient times. Nowadays, its delightful coves and beaches are much visited by scuba divers. For details of courses or information for certified divers, contact **Dive Med College** (❶ 22410 61115 Ⓦ www.divemedcollege.com).

Katharas Bay (popular with nudists) has a sandy shoreline but steep rocky terrain to the rear. Scenic **Anthony Quinn Bay** is a must-see, an inlet nestled between two mountains with rock formations jutting out into the sapphire waters. **Ladiko Bay** is a rocky cove with attractions such as the 'Seal's Cave' and the ancient fortress of Erimokastro.

RESTAURANTS & BARS

Chaplins € Lively beach bar, serving cocktails and snacks throughout the day. Theme nights and DJs. ⓐ Faliraki Square ❶ 22410 85662 Ⓦ www.chaplins.net ◐ Open 09.00–03.00

Dimitra €€ Greek taverna with over 500 menu items. Situated on the beach ⓐ Faliraki Square ◐ Open 09.00–midnight

⬆ *Faliraki offers a full range of water sports*

Golden Wok €€ Red lanterns and dragons decorate this recently opened eatery. Great for families as there is lots of elbow room! ⓐ Rhodes–Lindos Road ⓣ 22410 86143 ⓛ Open 17.00–midnight

Opera Restaurant €€ Beautiful atrium-style restaurant on three levels offering excellent international cuisine. ⓐ Kalithea Avenue ⓣ 22410 85776 ⓛ Open 18.00–midnight

Underground € A family pub with pool tables, swings and karaoke, serving huge portions of English food including Sunday roasts. ⓐ Lido Road ⓣ 22410 86831 ⓛ Open 09.00–03.00

NIGHTLIFE
Bedrock Party prehistoric style with a Flintstones theme disco. DJ spins 60s, 70s, 80s and 90s tunes from a dinosaur egg. ⓐ Kalithea Avenue ⓛ Open 20.00–late

The Castle Excellent nightclub in a castle, with a spectacular view of Faliraki. On three levels, pool bar with live bands, disco and jazz bar. More mature crowd than a typical Faliraki bar. ⓐ Rhodes–Lindos Avenue (just past the traffic lights, atop the hill on the right) ⓛ Open 23.00–late

Maze This huge club holds over 3500 people and is the main Rhodes for big-name DJs. Music suits all tastes and ages. ⓐ Off Kalithea Avenue ⓛ Open midnight–04.00

SHOPPING
Musses (ⓐ Faliraki Shopping Centre) has a selection of dried nuts and fruits, sweets, coffees and chocolates, sold by weight. Also try **Sky Ice Cream Parlour** (ⓐ Across the road from SkySurfer ⓛ Open 18.00–midnight).

⬤ *Afandou beach is one of the finest stretches of sand on the island*

Afandou
the invisible village

Afandou (pronounced 'Ofan-doo') was deliberately built out of sight of the sea to protect it from marauding pirates (the name means 'invisible village'). That said, the main attraction of the resort today is the 7 km (4¹/₂ mile) long Blue Flag beach, one of the finest expanses of sand and pebbles on the island.

There is more to the 'invisible village' than meets the eye. Af
andou's cultural heritage is on show in the beautifully decorated parish church and in a small museum in the grounds (🕒 Open 10.00–noon 🛈 Admission charge). One room features a typical kitchen sideboard with hand-painted ceramic plates, traditional wooden utensils and an old-fashioned loom with examples of hand-woven carpets; in the other room are displays of precious religious objects including vestments, silver chalices, bibles and painted icons.

While strolling through the village look out for old women wearing the hand-painted headscarves for which Afandou was once famous and take a peep into the courtyards of the houses behind Pernou Street. These are still used as second living rooms by many people (some villagers even sleep here on hot summer nights).

Fun for the kids, the **tourist train** also saves grown-ups a 3 km (2 mile) walk to the beach. It departs from the centre of the village throughout the day, with additional stops at the Afandou Beach Hotel, the Lippia Hotel and the golf course. It continues around the village and resort (but not the beach) until 23.00.

THINGS TO SEE & DO
Cycling ★
Cycling is a great way to get about and explore neighbouring resorts. Bikes can be hired from the **Motor Center**. ⓐ 49 Pernou St (opposite Moka) 📞 22410 51507 🕒 Open 08.30–13.00 and 17.00–23.00

Golf ★

Afandou's 18-hole championship course (par 73), designed by British golf architect David Harradine, is Rhodes' only course. Pros rate it as challenging but fair. It has a clubhouse with bar, changing rooms and equipment hire. The Rodos Open is held here in October. ☎ 22410 51451 ⓦ www.afandougolfcourse.com 🕐 Open all year 07.30–20.00

Working out ★

The **Body Work** gym has an impressive range of aerobic machines and a sauna. ⓐ 2 Valetsiou Street ☎ 22410 52570 🕐 Open Mon–Fri 10.00–22.00, Sat 11.00–20.00 ❶ Credit cards accepted

EXCURSIONS
Butterfly Valley ★★★

Drive across country to enjoy the natural beauty of **Petaloudes**, a scenic gorge which, from May to September, is home to the eyecatching but rare Jersey Tiger moths. There are shady walks through the woods and restaurant tables overlooking the waterfall and stream (page 33).

RESTAURANTS

Golfer Restaurant €€ A shady terrace restaurant serving home-made specialities. Try the fried vegetables *à la maison*, moussaka or 'hole in one' – roast lamb rolled in filo pastry. ⓐ Rhodes–Lindos Road, opposite the entrance to the Golf Course ☎ 22410 51861 🕐 Open Mon 17.00–midnight and Tues–Sun 11.00–23.00

Life Garden €€ Set apart from the main Pernou Street, this family-orientated restaurant serves Italian, Greek and English fare. A helpful menu lists the ingredients of the traditional Greek dishes. ⓐ Pernou Street ☎ 22410 52422 🕐 Open 18.30–23.30

Michalis € Informal Greek restaurant offering English breakfast as well as pork chops, mixed grills and kebabs. ⓐ 125 Pernou Street ☎ 22410 51387 🕐 Open 09.00–15.00 and 18.00–midnight

Reni €€€ Serves delicious fresh fish and grilled meats. This is a great place, overlooking the sea, to watch the sunset over evening cocktails. **ⓐ** On the beach **ⓣ** 22410 51280 **ⓛ** Open 11.00–02.00

Sergios €€ Watch the world go by from the romantic roof-garden while enjoying the mixture of Italian and Greek dishes. Air conditioning and satellite TV. **ⓐ** 3 Pernou Street **ⓣ** 22410 52050 **ⓛ** Open 18.00–midnight

NIGHTLIFE

Cream Club Party till the wee hours of the morning while enjoying luscious cocktails and great music. **ⓐ** Plateau Goumerobox **ⓛ** Open 23.00–late

Day and Night Listen to international and Greek music as you relax with an evening cocktail. **ⓐ** 36 Pernou Street **ⓣ** 22410 52509 **ⓛ** Open 09.00–01.00

Diva Club/Garden This lively club appeals to locals and visitors with a mix of disco and Greek music. It also has a garden bar making it great for hot evenings. **ⓐ** 148 Pernou Street **ⓣ** 22410 52300 **ⓛ** Open 17.00–06.00

SHOPPING

The main shopping street is Pernou where you'll find a pharmacy, several well-stocked supermarkets, souvenir shops, travel agents, a small CD outlet, sports outfitters and several restaurants. The **Kamara gallery** sells handmade pottery, model fishing boats and other Greek souvenirs. Gold and silver jewellery can be found at **Irinis Gold. Alko** (**ⓐ** 53 Pernou Street) has a good selection of local wines. **Gelateria Moka** (**ⓐ** also on Pernou Street), sells delicious Greek sweets and pastries, like baklava, as well as coffee.

Kolymbia
smart purpose-built resort

**Eucalyptus trees shade the main avenue of Kolymbia (pronounced
'Ko-lim-ba'), a smart, purpose-built resort overlooking Afandou bay.
The beach consists of a long stretch of fine golden sand ending at
Vagia Point, a small cove ringed by volcanic rock. Kolymbia itself has an
assortment of shops and restaurants and regular buses run throughout
the day to Afandou, Rhodes Town and Lindos.**

 As Kolymbia is a relatively peaceful resort, night owls make for
the bright lights of Faliraki, a short taxi ride away.

Beyond Kolymbia the mountain road climbs to the local beauty spot,
Epta Piges ('seven springs'). Italian engineers built a reservoir here in
the 1930s – the waterfall in the centre of Kolymbia is part of the same
irrigation project. The original stream flowing from the springs has been
diverted through a dank and rather spooky 170 m (186 yds) long tunnel

🔻 *Kolymbia overlooks Afandou bay*

to the man-made lake – if you're brave enough, you can wade ankle-deep in the icy water. If you prefer to stay above ground, there is an alternative route to the reservoir following a rugged footpath through the pine forest. The scenic taverna attracts the crowds, especially at lunchtime.

A quieter spot is the little mountain village of **Arhipoli**, just 5 km (3 miles) further up the road where you can relax over a glass of *suma*, the potent local firewater.

THINGS TO SEE & DO
Archangelos ★★

The largest village on Rhodes, Archangelos is still relatively unspoilt by tourism and has retained many ancient customs and traditions. The people speak their own dialect, and their distinctive leather boots (which can be worn on either foot), have been specially adapted to give protection from snakes (you can buy a pair to take home if you can spare the time for a fitting). Alternatively, the local pottery workshops produce hand-painted plates decorated with traditional motifs. Archangelos is famous for its oranges (sold mainly in winter and spring) but you'll also see groves of lemons, figs, vines and olives growing beneath the ruins of the 15th-century castle.

Lindos ★★★

A day excursion to Lindos (page 49) might include a donkey ride to the **Temple of Athena** on the Acropolis, a leisurely stroll through the mosaic-paved streets and alleyways, a stop for lunch at one of the former seafarers' houses and a cooling swim at one of the two village beaches. The **Kolymbia Express boat** leaves daily (except Mon) from the harbour at 09.30, stopping en route to Lindos for a swim. It returns to Kolymbia at 16.00.

Mini-golf ★

Try the mini-golf in the pretty garden of **Kolimpia Star**, a popular café.
➌ Near Hotel Tropical ❶ 22410 56309 ❷ Open 10.00–01.00, or later

SHOPPING

Most of the shops are located in Eucalyptus Avenue. **Kolymbia Gold** and **Irene Gold** sell jewellery while **Mega Market** stocks sportswear. **Art Line** has a good range of casual clothes, including baseball hats. The **Brillante complex** includes a mini-market and souvenir shops and **Fleranis supermarket** is a useful port of call for those on self-catering holidays. For arty postcards or a souvenir painting of Greece, try the **Art Gallery**.

Tsampika ★ ★

The hilltop monastery takes its name from the *tsampas* (sparks) which lit up the sky when an icon from a church on Cyprus miraculously materialized on Rhodes. (The Cypriots reclaimed the icon three times but it kept returning until they eventually let it be.) Every year, on 8 September, local women make a pilgrimage to Tsampika to pray for fertility. If their prayers are answered with a boy, he is called Tsampikos; if a girl, Tsampika. There are commanding views of the coast from the monastery, while the beach below is unspoilt and ideal for sun-worshippers.

BEACHES

There are two main beaches – one by **To Nissaki restaurant** and the other by **Limanaki restaurant**. Both are gently shelving, perfect for swimming and safe for children. Sunbeds, umbrellas and pedalos can be hired, but water sports enthusiasts and thrill seekers are better served in Afandou (5 km/3 miles) where you can hire pedalos and water-ski, or try Faliraki (10 km/6 miles) where catamaran sailing and paragliding are available as well.

RESTAURANTS & BARS

Brillantina € This café-bar with a cool, shady terrace, in the Brillante shopping centre, also serves pizzas and delicious ice cream.

ⓐ Eucalyptus Avenue ⓣ 22410 56369 ⓞ Open 11.00–midnight, or later

Carrusel € A cheap and cheerful Greek restaurant with a menu in English. Try the chicken *souvlaki* and the *gyros*. ⓐ Eucalyptus Avenue ❶ 22410 56085 ◷ Open 11.00–midnight

Limanaki €€ Come to this bright blue taverna with its ornamental fish tanks and waterfalls, for good food, beautiful views over the coastline and the best sunsets in Kolymbia. ⓐ Limanaki beach ❶ 22410 56240 ◷ Open 09.00 for drinks, midday for food, closes 01.00, or later

To Nissaki €€ A simple bar and taverna right on the beach. Try the mixed fish platter washed down with Rhodian wine from the village of Empona. ⓐ Kolymbia beach ❶ 22410 56360 ◷ Open 11.00–midnight, or later (bar 10.00–midnight)

Panoramic €€ Standing 300 m (985 ft) high above the resort, this rustic restaurant serves local dishes and home-made bread, while you experience the most magical views across the interior of Rhodes. ⓐ Tsampika monastery ❶ (mobile) 62460 61262 ◷ Open 09.00–20.00

Savvas €€ The speciality in this Greek restaurant is a mouth-watering and bargain-priced mixed grill (for two persons). ⓐ Eucalyptus Avenue ❶ 22410 56300 ◷ Open 11.00–22.00

Vagios €€ This large, air-conditioned restaurant welcomes families. The extensive menu (in Greek and German) includes pizzas, *gyros*, fish, octopus and steaks. ⓐ Eucalyptus Avenue ❶ 22410 56006 ◷ Open 18.00–midnight

NIGHTLIFE

Memories The large-screen TV is a popular feature here. Cocktails are '2 for the price of 1' in the early evening. ⓐ Eucalyptus Avenue ❶ 22410 56502 ◷ Open 16.00–01.00

Lindos
island heritage

St Paul visited Lindos in AD 58 and found a wealthy and prosperous community with a history stretching back at least 1500 years. The Acropolis, with its ruined Temple of Athena, is the jewel in the crown of this Grade 1 archaeological site, where cars and bikes are outlawed and the only means of transport is by donkey. Visitors can enjoy a drink in one of the old seafarers' houses, admire the local pottery and needlework on display in the narrow cobbled streets and take a cooling dip in the bay.

All signs in Lindos point to the **Acropolis** (📞 22440 31258 🕐 Open Tues–Sun 08.00–18.30). Resist the temptation to buy 'traditional' embroidery along the way – most of it is imported and overpriced. At the foot of the **Knights' Staircase** (leading to the castle) is a large relief of a trireme (the ancient Greek sailing ship) which was carved out of the rock in the 2nd century BC.

The Knights built their stronghold on the foundations of the classical city, so today visitors can see the remains of both. Look out for the lofty chambers of the commander's palace, the remaining columns of an 87 m (95 yds) long portico and the regal flight of steps leading to the ruined 4th-century-AD **Temple of Athena** (patron goddess of Lindos). From here there are fabulous views over **Pallas beach** in one direction and the azure-blue waters of **St Paul's Bay** in the other.

The most novel way of approaching the Acropolis is by donkey (the so-called 'Lindos taxi'). If you pay extra, you can have a photograph as a souvenir.

◀ *St Paul's Bay has beautiful azure-blue waters*

THINGS TO SEE & DO
Boat trips ★★
Catch the once-weekly boat to Rhodes Town for some shopping. Alternatively, climb aboard one of the daily excursion boats which explore the south-eastern coast, with swimming stops.

Captain's House ★★
Many local seafarers' houses, similar to this one, date from the 16th and 17th centuries, and have now been converted to restaurants and bars. Look out for the tell-tale features: rope coils and other nautical motifs on doorways, painted ceramic plates hanging from the interior walls (kept as souvenirs of voyages) and balconied courtyards with distinctive pebble mosaic floors known as *choklaki*. **Captain's House Bar**, now a classical music bar, can be seen en route to the Acropolis.

ⓐ 243 Acropolis Street ⓣ 22440 31235 ⓛ Open 08.00–early morning

Church of the Assumption ★★
The red-tiled domes and elegant bell tower of this delightful Byzantine church are a local landmark. In the 18th century the walls, ceilings – and even the pulpit – were covered with frescoes. The vivid *Last Judgement* on the back wall was a reminder to all of their mortality.

ⓛ Open 09.00–noon and 16.00–19.00

EXCURSIONS
Charaki ★★
This attractive fishing village (pronounced 'Har-aki'), north of Lindos, is now a developing resort. A steep climb from the beach is the formidable castle of **Feraklos**, the last stronghold on the island to be captured by the Turks.

BEACHES
Water-skiing, pedalos and parascending are all available from the small **Pallas** beach in Main Bay, where there is also a roped-off safe area for children. Sunbeds and parasols are also available in **St Paul's Bay**.

SHOPPING

Lindian pottery was once a collector's item. The ceramic plates, decorated with traditional motifs of flowers, swirling leaves and of course, ships, make attractive souvenirs. Handmade thonged sandals are another speciality, as are belts, rucksacks, wallets and handbags. Shops that sell gifts to take home include **Sokaki Gift Shop**, **Lindos Gold and Silver** and **Makris Ceramics**.

○ *View of Lindos across Main Bay*

RESTAURANTS & BARS (see map below)

Alex's Taverna €€ ❶ This fish restaurant is right by the beach.
ⓐ Pallas beach ❸ 22440 31473 ● Open 09.00–21.00, or last customer

Aphrodite €€ ❷ Attractive fish restaurant with roof-garden, popular with local residents. International cuisine. ⓐ Acropolis Street ❸ 22440 31255 ● Open 18.00–23.30

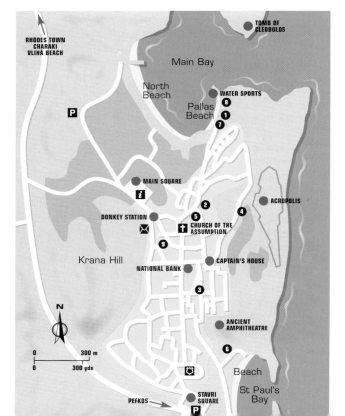

Bacco Luna Bar € ❸ Delicious international cuisine in the heart of Lindos. Roof garden and music. ☎ 22440 31431 🕐 Open 17.00–01.00

Caesar's Restaurant €€ ❹ Half-way up to the Acropolis, this is a great place to stop for juice or a light snack in the day, or a romantic meal in the evening on the vine-clad patio or roof-terrace. Traditional Greek cuisine. ⓐ Acropolis Street ☎ 22440 31410 🕐 Open 08.00–01.00

Cyprus Taverna €€€ ❺ Also known as Timi's Place, this restaurant serves Cypriot specialities, like *seftalies* (grilled mincemeat with spices), plus chicken and fish dishes. ⓐ 191 Acropolis Street ☎ 22440 31539 🕐 Open 11.00–14.45 and 18.00–23.00

Il Palazzetto €€€ ❻ A beautiful Italian-owned restaurant set around a courtyard for delectable pasta, meat and fish dishes, and pizzas cooked in wood ovens. ⓐ Near St Paul's Bay and Amphitheatre ☎ 22440 31612 🕐 Open 18.00–midnight

 Pallas Taverna € ❼ Delicious Greek food is served in this beachfront restaurant together with burgers, pizzas, toasties and take-aways. ⓐ Pallas beach ☎ 22440 31433 🕐 Open 09.00–21.30

Rainbird Bar € ❽ Breakfast and snacks 09.00–16.00; thereafter, drinks only. ⓐ Pallas beach ☎ 22440 31869 🕐 Open 09.00–03.00

NIGHTLIFE

Lindos has four nightclubs. **Medusa** and **Arch Club** are centrally located indoor discos while **Amphitheatre** and **Acropolis** are open-air and more peripheral. They all start at around midnight and continue until dawn.

Lindos by Night ❾ Probably the liveliest bar in town, situated on three different levels to suit all moods: the romantic rooftop terrace; the fountain bar with its amazing jungle of plants and waterfalls; and the lower bar with a mix of music. ☎ 22440 31463 🕐 Open 19.00–02.00

Pefkos, Lardos & Kiotari
relaxing southern resorts

The developing southern resorts of Pefkos, Lardos and Kiotari are best known for their leisurely pace of life and their often deserted beaches. Their low-key nightlife is centred around traditional tavernas and the friendly bars, although the more lively nightlife of Lindos is never far away.

Set amidst pine trees in a picturesque bay just 5 km (3 miles) south of the busy resort of Lindos, **Pefkos** (meaning 'pine tree') was once the Lindians' summer hide-away. Now it is a popular, laid-back resort in its own right, with smart new holiday accommodation and a good selection of restaurants, shops and bars scattered along the main road and on the street leading to its long, sandy beach. From here, a daily ferry boat whisks shoppers and sightseers to Lindos, leaving at 10.00 and returning to Pefkos at 16.30.

South of Pefkos, the popular international resort of **Lardos** (the name perhaps deriving from the rocky ground known as 'Lartian stone,' or meaning 'pigfat') is centred on a traditional Greek village, set in beautiful, unspoilt countryside 2 km (1 mile) inland. With a wide variety of sand-and-pebble beaches, coves and rocky inlets to choose from on the stretch of coast between Pefkos and Lardos, an excellent range of water sports, and a go-karting track on the village outskirts, the village is quite sleepy during the day. By night, however, village life centres around an array of traditional tavernas, fish restaurants and bars in the main square.

Further south, the newly developed resort of **Kiotari** is another relaxed and spacious alternative to the bustle of nearby Lindos, with a long, shingle beach, a handful of shorefront tavernas and extensive water sports facilities. As with Pefkos and Lardos, Kiotari makes an ideal base from which to explore the quieter southern half of the island and its lesser-known beaches.

THINGS TO SEE & DO

Prassonissi ★★

Prassonissi or 'Leek Island' marks Rhodes' southernmost extremity, where the Aegean Sea meets the Mediterranean – a paradise for windsurfers. From May to September it is possible to stroll across the broad, sandy causeway that links Prassonissi to the rest of Rhodes, but during winter it is cut off by high seas.

Thari Monastery ★★

The oldest surviving religious foundation on Rhodes has recently been re-established and the 9th-century monastery church is open to the public. Glorious frescoes of the Apostles and the prophets cover the apse and dome while, in the nave, unusual biblical scenes are depicted, such as the storm on the Sea of Galilee. ◐ Open 10.00–18.00

Water sports ★

The **Lardos Skiing and Fun Centre** at St George's Hotel (ⓐ Aghios Georgios) offers water-skiing and parasailing or go to **Watersports Centre Kiotari** (ⓐ Kiotari beach) for windsurfing, parasailing and water-skiing.

RESTAURANTS & BARS

Coralli €€ There's something for everyone here: local cuisine, a pretty pool overlooking the beach, delicious cocktails and entertainment nights. ⓐ Pefkos–Lardos Road, Lardos ⓣ 22440 48066 ◐ Open 09.00–01.00

Greek House €€ Try the range of fantastic *crêpes*, or stop in for delicious Greek cuisine of grilled meats or fish. ⓐ Pefkos beach ⓣ 22440 48167 ◐ Open 11.30–23.30

Kelari Bar €€ Relax to great music in this bar specializing in a range of cocktails, beers and spirits. ⓐ 100 m (109 yds) from Pefkos beach ⓣ 22440 48357 ◐ Open 17.00–03.00

Lardos Charcoal Broil € Tiny, cheap locals' café specializing in *souvlaki, gyros* and spit-roasted chicken. ⓐ Main square, Lardos ❶ 22440 44350 ❶ Open noon–01.00

 Monrella €€ The best taverna in Kiotari serves excellent local cuisine with smiling service. ⓐ Kiotari beach ❶ Open noon–22.30

La Piazza €€ Lively Italian restaurant, also sells take-away pizzas and pasta. ⓐ Pefkos–Lardos road, Pefkos ❶ 22440 48295 ❶ Open 17.00–midnight

Shanghai € Done with kebabs and moussaka? Try this excellent Chinese restaurant – it also offers a variety of vegetarian dishes. ⓐ Pefkos–Lardos Road, Pefkos ❶ 22440 48217 ❶ Open 18.00–midnight

Stefano €€ Try the grilled octopus, prawns or seafood platter at this simple fish restaurant, overlooking a tiny fishing harbour. ⓐ Kiotari beach ❶ 22440 47339 ❶ Open noon–23.00

NIGHTLIFE

Pefkos by Night is a lively bar in Pefkos, although **Nostalgia Restaurant Bar**, with swimming pool and roof garden, and **Eclipse** are also extremely popular. In Lardos, **Memories** music bar is the place to meet in the evenings for cocktails.

⬤ *Lardos is set in beautiful, unspoilt countryside*

RESORTS
Kos

Kos Town
blend of ancient and modern

The capital of Kos island is an attractive and lively port, with shady tree-lined avenues and lush green spaces brightened by lilac, jasmine and hibiscus. Kos town's sights include two mosques, a medieval castle and ancient remains, most notably the Asklepion, perhaps Europe's oldest health resort. The beaches offer a variety of water sports, while boat excursions leave from the harbour for the neighbouring islands.

A miniature train (the **Dotto train**) takes visitors on a 15-minute whistle-stop tour of the town centre, departing from the harbour at half-hourly intervals from 10.00 to 14.00 and 18.00 to 20.00.

Guarding the port, and its clutter of yachts and motor vessels, is the **Castle of the Knights of St John**, built in the 14th and 15th centuries with a massive outer wall and keep which look impregnable even today (🕐 Open Tues–Sun 08.30–14.30 ❶ Admission charge). Alongside is an avenue lined with palm trees; this was originally the moat, which separated the castle from the town.

Nearby, you will find **Hippocrates' plane tree**. It may not really have sheltered the ancient Greek physician, but it is at least 700 years old and boasts a trunk 17 m (19 yds) in circumference. Overlooking the tree is an 18th-century **Turkish mosque** and, nearby, the ruins of the *agora*, a market-cum-shopping arcade, dating back to the 4th century BC. Today's shoppers head for the fruit and vegetable market in Eleftherias Square and the pedestrianized 'Old Bazaar' on Ifestou Street.

THINGS TO SEE & DO
Archaeological treasures ★★
The town centre contains the ruins of the Roman agora (market), a running track, an amphitheatre and the **Casa Romana**, a restored Roman

◀ *Kos Town is a site full of ancient remains*

villa containing fine mosaics and murals (currently closed for repairs but due to re-open in 2006). Further treasures can be seen in **Kos Museum** (ⓐ Eleftherias Square ❶ 22420 28326 ❶ Open Tues–Sun 08.00–14.30 ❶ Admission charge), including an ancient statue of Hippocrates and a beautiful mosaic of Hippocrates welcoming Asklepios to Kos.

Orfeas ★
This is an open-air cinema which often shows English-language films during the summer – details are posted up in Eleftherias Square.

Go-kart racing ★
There is a track just west of the town at Psalidi. ⓐ Main road, Psalidi ❶ 22420 25897 ❶ Open 09.00–23.00

Scuba diving ★
Kos Diving Centre organizes everything from international PADI courses for beginners to expert deep, night and drift dives. ⓐ 7 Achillea Pasanikolaki Street ❶ Open 10.00–20.00

BEACHES
The **town beach**, east of the harbour, becomes crowded very early in the day. A better bet, also called **Town Beach**, is about 500 m (550 yds) west of the centre (bus no. 2) where you can windsurf or paraglide. There are

HIPPOCRATES
According to legend, the famous Greek physician was born on Kos around 460 BC. The 'father of Western medicine' encouraged his followers to observe patients' symptoms, rather than attributing all illness to the wrath of the gods. The **Asklepion**, one of more than 200 shrines built, is among the most famous in the world, and is dedicated to the god of healing – Asklepios.

plenty of tavernas and snack bars nearby, and it is close to the discos and water facilities. For somewhere quieter and less congested, head for **Tingaki**, a little further west, or **Psalidi** on the other side of town (bus no. 1). Both have water sports facilities. Beyond Psalidi, **Aghios Fokas** beach has volcanic black sand and is often deserted.

 A Greek guardsmen's military band marches through the town and around the harbourfront every Sunday evening.

EXCURSIONS
Asklepion ★★
Dedicated to Asklepios, the Greek god of healing, this ancient medical centre, which comprised hostels, baths, temples and recovery rooms, followed the teachings of Hippocrates, who was born on Kos in the 5th century BC (doctors still take the Hippocratic Oath today). There are superb views from the pine-clad hill high above the town. The **Dotto train** leaves Kos Harbour at half-hourly intervals from 10.00 to 14.00 hours and 18.00 to 20.00 hours (journey time 20 minutes). ● Open Tues–Fri 08.00–19.00, Sat and Sun 08.00–14.30 (last entrance 30 minutes before closing) ❶ Admission charge

Platani ★★
A charming village on the outskirts of Kos Town, where Greek Orthodox people live peacefully together with Muslims of Turkish descent. It is also a popular lunch stop on the way back from the Asklepion.

Psalidi ★★
Psalidi is really just an extension of Kos Town, a peaceful overflow of hotels, bars and waterfront restaurants. Its real attraction, however, is the hot spring of **Bros Therma**, which runs directly into the sea 5 km (3 miles) beyond **Aghios Fokas** beach, where you can bathe away your aches and pains in the warm sulphuric spring water in a man-made rock pool at the water's edge.

RESTAURANTS (see map above)

Anatolia Hamam €€€ ❶ A beautiful restaurant, housed in the ancient *hamam* (bath-house). Specialities include rabbit *stifado* (stew) and pork fillet with plum sauce. The wine list is impressive and there is a children's menu too. ➌ 3 Nissiriou (behind Diagoras Square) ☎ 22420 28323 ⏰ Open 09.00–midnight

Boomerang €€ ❷ Lively Australian restaurant with extensive international menu. Backs on to the popular Irish karaoke bar, Shananagans. ➌ Mandilara ☎ 22420 28394 ⏰ Open 09.00–midnight

Café Central € ❸ Stop at this friendly café near the market to enjoy a coffee, a refreshing fresh fruit juice, or a light snack under the shade of plane trees. The cheese pie with honey is especially tasty. ➌ 17 Vasileos Pavlou Street ☎ 22420 25302 ⏰ Open 08.00–22.00

Goody's € ❹ Greece's answer to McDonald's. ⓐ Bar Street ☎ 22420 25298 ⓦ www.goodys.com 🕐 Open 10.00–04.30; 10.00–06.00 Sat and Sun

Mavromattis €€ ❺ Jolly blue-and-white seafront taverna, well known for its fresh fish. Ask for a table on the beach. ⓐ Psalidi waterfront ☎ 22420 22433 🕐 Open 11.00–midnight

Otto e Mezzo €€€ ❻ The garden terrace of this top Italian restaurant makes a lovely setting for a romantic meal. Specialities include fresh pasta, grilled meats and mouth-watering home-made cakes. ⓐ 21 Apellou Street ☎ 22420 20069 🕐 Open 09.30–midnight; food served from noon

Passage to India €€ ❼ Authentic Indian cuisine, and the best baltis in town! ⓐ 55 Makrigianni Street ☎ 22420 21365 🕐 Open 18.00–midnight, or later

To Petrino €€€ ❽ This charming candlelit garden restaurant is known for its excellent *mezedes*, stuffed vegetables, and seafood dishes. ⓐ Theologou Square ☎ 22420 27251 🕐 Open 18.00–midnight

Spitaki €€ ❾ French and Italian cuisine, very tasty food. ⓐ Psalidi waterfront ☎ 22420 27655 🕐 Food served 11.00–16.00 and 19.00–midnight

Taverna Therma €€ ❿ One of the best fish restaurants in Kos, with a constantly changing menu according to the daily catch. ⓐ Down by the hot springs at Psalidi (remember to bring your swimsuit!) ☎ 69770 70744 🕐 Open 10.00–22.00

Theatraki € ⓫ In peaceful surroundings by ancient ruins this café serves quiches, salads, coffees and milkshakes by day, and cocktails by night ⓐ 5 Gregoriou ☎ 22420 25052 🕐 Open 08.00–01.00

 Kos Town offers a wide range of cafés and restaurants

NIGHTLIFE

Apoplous ⑫ This extremely up-market bouzouki club is owned by Kostas Kaiserlis, a local man. He has a resident orchestra and singers, and regularly invites guest artists from mainland Greece. ⓐ G Papandreou Street, Psalidi ⓣ 22420 21916 ⓛ Open midnight–05.00

Bluebird ⑬ A wonderfully romantic colonial-style bar, right on the water's edge. ⓐ G Papandreou Street, Psalidi ⓛ Open 18.30–02.00

Charisma Club ⑭ One of the better party bars in Kos Town ⓐ Bar Street ⓣ 22420 25298 ⓛ Open 20.30–04.00 (to 06.00 Fri and Sat)

Fashion ⑮ An amazing laser show makes this disco popular with tourists and young Greeks. The bar outside is popular during the early evening, with happy hour from 19.00 to 22.00. ⓐ 2 Kanari Street ⓣ 22420 22592 ⓛ Open midnight–06.00 (bar 19.00–23.00)

Four Roses ⑯ Bar/nightclub by the sea. Good music, popular with locals. ⓐ Vasileos Georgiou waterfront ⓣ 22420 21060 ⓛ Open 10.00–05.00

Haman ⓱ Bar set in an old Turkish bath, with occasional live music, plus Greek music and chart-topping hits. ⓐ 1 Akti Koundourioti ⓣ 22420 24938 ⓒ Open 21.00–04.00 (disco from midnight)

Heaven ⓲ Chic nightclub with tropical garden bar, swimming pool, and changing theme nights throughout the week. It is also open during the day for snacks and drinks. ⓐ Zouroudi Street, Lambi ⓣ 22420 23874 ⓒ Open 11.00–05.00

SHOPPING

The **central fruit and vegetable market** (ⓒ Open Mon–Sat 06.00–23.00, Sun 10.00–14.00 and 19.00–23.00) in Eleftherias Square also sells honey, Greek Delight and nuts. The shops surrounding the market sell ceramics, embroidery and other souvenirs. As drinks and wine are very inexpensive, there are many different shops throughout the town. Other useful shops are:

Athletes Foot Sells a wide range of leisure clothes and sports goods. ⓐ 6 Al Ipsilandou Street.

Bread Bazaar A bakery and patisserie. ⓐ 1 Ant. Ioannididi

Hercules For hand-painted ceramics, candles, soaps, shells and sponges. ⓐ 20 Apellou Street

Newsagency For international newspapers, magazines, books and maps on Kos. ⓐ 2 Riga Ferrou

Pure Silver and Argentum For good quality jewellery. ⓐ 1 and 7 Apellou Street

Saroukos Express For film developing and printing in one hour. ⓐ 1 Ifestou Street

Stohos For wine and spirits. ⓐ 15 Makrigianni Street

Theologos Romanas For leather clothing, bags, belts and wallets. ⓐ 12 Apellou Street

Ti Amo Music For modern and traditional Greek music. ⓐ El Venizelou Street

Tingaki
relaxing beach resort

Located on the northern coast of Kos, Tingaki (also known as Tigaki) is a mere 15 minutes from the nightlife of Kos Town, but offers a more relaxed pace for those who prefer quiet evenings and a peaceful environment. With its sheltered Blue Flag beach, Tingaki is also the perfect destination for families.

Once a humble fishing village, Tingaki is now a small, pleasant resort with a handful of medium-sized hotels and attractive apartment blocks scattered amongst fields along the coast. Its long, tree-fringed beach of coarse, white sand is one of the finest on the island, with sunbeds and parasols supplied, and an excellent variety of water sports. The outlines of **Kalymnos** and **Pserimos** islands and Turkey's **Bodrum Peninsula** on the horizon provide a spectacular backdrop.

Tingaki is also the perfect base from which to explore inland, where the countryside is unexpectedly lush and fertile, and its narrow lanes bright with flowers and pretty houses. Unlike many Greek islands, Kos receives a fair amount of seasonal rain, hence the many cultivated fields of fruit and vegetables, orange and olive groves, vineyards and, of course, the island's best-known produce – Cos lettuce.

For a change of scene, take the winding mountain road through the cluster of five villages, collectively known as **Asfendiou**, where the whitewashed houses clinging to the slopes of **Mount Dikaio** are sheltered from the sun by forests, fruit and walnut groves. **Zia** has the best views and also makes a good lunch stop, though at times the crowds can be tiresome.

'Greek evenings' are held in the tavernas round the village square in Zia. Watch the sun set over the Aegean, then enjoy a traditional Greek meal, washed down with local wine and accompanied by singing and dancing. Ask your holiday representative for further details.

THINGS TO SEE & DO

Cycling ★

Hire a bike for the day to explore the surrounding countryside or to cycle into Kos Town. If you're feeling really energetic, you could head inland to the Asklepion or to some of the island's beautiful mountain villages. Both **Euro Duck** (❶ 22420 69080 ● Open 10.00–20.00) and **Manolis** (❶ 22420 69230 ● Open 10.00–19.00) rent bicycles and scooters.

Go-karting ★

Providing fun for all the family, **Christos Go-Karting** track has special mini-karts for children as young as two. There's also a small bar serving snacks. ❸ Marmari main road ❶ 22420 68184 ● Open 09.30–23.00

Horse riding ★

The **Marmari Riding Centre** on Kos offers a variety of guided riding excursions for children and adults of all levels: one-hour rides to the beach (at 10.00, 11.00, noon, 16.00, 17.00 and 18.00), or three-hour treks into the mountains (on Thurs at 10.00, and to Mastichari on Fri at 10.00 hours). ❸ Half-way between Tingaki and Marmari ❶ (mobile) 6944 104446

Water sports ★

A wide variety of water sports is available on the beach near Tingaki Square, including water-skiing, sailing, windsurfing and pedalos. **Watersports Xtreme** ❸ Kos Town beach ❶ 69445 74347 ● Open 10.00–17.00

EXCURSIONS

Island hopping ★ ★ ★

If you fancy exploring further afield during your stay, **Tingaki Tours** organize regular excursions to Kalymnos (page 90), Nisyros (page 88), Bodrum (page 85) and Rhodes (page 14). ❸ Tingaki Square ❶ 22420 69494 ● Open 10.00–20.00

Mountain villages ★★★

The unspoilt Asfendiou villages – **Amaniou**, **Evangelistria**, **Lagoudi**, **Pyli** and **Zia** – clustered on the fertile slopes of **Mount Dikaio**, provide a rare glimpse of rural island life before tourism took hold. Evangelistria is especially picturesque, with its low, whitewashed houses, attractive Byzantine church and popular taverna (see below). Zia, the highest village on Kos, is more developed, with several excellent restaurants (see below) and souvenir shops. The countryside is popular for walking and there is a **riding centre** in Amaniou (ⓦ www.alfa-horse.com). One footpath leads from the village to the summit of Mount Dikaio (846 m/2775 ft), passing the Kefalovrysi church – a three-hour climb.

SHOPPING

Useful shops in Tingaki include **Katerina Supermarket and Tourist Shop** (ⓐ Main road ● 08.30–22.30), a one-stop convenience store at the heart of the resort for food, drink, papers and magazines, books, beachwear, buckets and spades, and souvenirs. On the outskirts, **Konstantinos hypermarket** (● Open Mon–Sat 08.00–22.30) is especially handy for those in self-catering. It also stocks leatherware, clothing and souvenirs. For reasonably priced jewellery, try **The Gold Shop** (ⓐ Main road ● Open 10.00–19.00).

RESTAURANTS

Asfendiou € This charming taverna in picturesque Evangelistria serves a simple menu of hearty local dishes, such as stuffed cabbage leaves or beef stew. Excellent value. ⓐ Evangelistria main square ① 22420 68679 ● Open 08.00–20.30

Avli €€ Traditional Greek cuisine with sensational views. Try the oven-roasted lamb or stuffed vine leaves. ⓐ Zia main square ① 22420 69185 ● Open 07.30–01.00

To Bouno €€ The place to watch the setting sun in Zia, To Bouno serves a wide variety of international dishes and good-value daily specials. ⓐ Zia main square ⓣ 22420 69066 ⓛ Open 08.00–01.00

Dana € The oldest restaurant in Tingaki is still one of the most popular. On the beach, with free use of sunbeds. ⓐ Tingaki seafront ⓣ 22420 69077 ⓛ Open 09.00–midnight

Esperos € Large, family restaurant right by the beach. Greek, vegetarian and international dishes, great local wines, and indoor and outdoor play areas. ⓐ Coastal road ⓣ 22420 69753 ⓛ Open 09.00–midnight

Olympia Taverna €€ The only restaurant in Zia without a view but reputedly one of the best tavernas on the island. The stuffed vine leaves and sausage and pepper stew are especially recommended. ⓐ Zia (upper quarter of the village) ⓣ 22420 69121 ⓛ Open 09.30–01.00

Plori €€ With wonderful sea views and fairy lights at night, this restaurant specializes in fish but also offers meat, pasta and other dishes. ⓐ Tingaki ⓣ 22420 69686 ⓛ Open 10.00–midnight

Tingaki Restaurant € Traditional taverna, à la carte or set menus. ⓐ Tingaki main square ⓣ 22420 69951 ⓛ Open 09.30–23.00

NIGHTLIFE

There are three bars on Tingaki's main road: **Memories cocktail bar**, open late; **Jungle Bar**, with chart and Greek music; and the lively disco bar **Mascot**.

🔻 *Enjoy the local cuisine*

Marmari & Mastichari
beautiful sandy coastline

The two fishing villages of Marmari and Mastichari on the north coast of Kos have been developed into peaceful, spacious seaside resorts. Both have broad, sandy beaches backed by sand dunes, and various shops, tavernas and bars, attracting couples and families in search of relaxation and a taste of traditional Greece.

The highlight of Marmari is undoubtedly its magnificent Blue Flag beach of golden sand and shingle. Windsurfing is popular here, and there is also horse riding and go-karting on the outskirts of the resort.

Mastichari is probably the least developed of the northern shore resorts. Its beach is sandy and stretches for miles, with the small, secluded beach of **Troulos** just 1 km (½ mile) to the east, reached by a dirt track. Village life centres on the fishing harbour, lined with the tiny fishing *caiques* which provide fresh fish on the tables of the dozen or so tavernas. It is also an important ferry port for **Kalymnos**, the island of the sponge fishermen (page 90), with boats sailing there several times a day, as well as to the tiny nearby island of **Pserimos**.

Marmari and Mastichari are popular with both walkers and cyclists eager to explore the island's hinterland. The charming mountain village of **Pyli**, centred around a tiny square with appealing craft shops and restaurants makes a good lunchtime destination. Three kilometres (2 miles) to the north and perched precariously on a craggy outcrop is **Paleo Pyli**, once the ancient capital of Kos. Now all that remains is a ruined Byzantine castle containing the 11th-century church of Ypapanti (Presentation).

Why not spend a day sightseeing in Kos Town? There are several buses a day from Marmari to Kos Town, providing the ideal opportunity to explore and shop for souvenirs to take home.

◀ *Marmari's fine beach of golden sand and shingle*

SHOPPING

In Mastichari, try **Gitonia** for herbs, hand-carved wood, pottery, carpets and Greek music; **Ira** and **Pia** for traditional gold and silverware; **Katepina** for leather goods and clothing; and **Mini-Market Australia** for Greek wines and general provisions. On the outskirts of Marmari is the **Konstantinos hypermarket** (🕒 Open Mon–Sat 08.00–22.30). For gifts, **Art Gallery Pyli** (📍 Just behind Pyli village square 📞 22420 41745) makes exclusive silver and gold jewellery, while **The Mermaid**, opposite, sells striking ceramics.

THINGS TO SEE & DO

Basilica ★

Take a walk to the western end of Mastichari beach to see the remains of a 5th-century basilica, Áyious Ioánnis.

Windsurfing ★

The **Fanatic Board Centre** at the western end of the resort rents out wetsuits, boards and other windsurfing equipment, as well as providing lessons for beginners. 📍 Marmari beach

RESTAURANTS & BARS

Apostolis €€ A lively taverna, notable *souvlaki* dishes and wines. 📍 Marmari main road 📞 22420 41403 🕒 Open 10.00–midnight

El Greco € This popular beach restaurant serves everything from cooked breakfasts to speciality barbecued steaks and swordfish. 📍 Mastichari beach 📞 22420 59112 🕒 Open 08.30–midnight

Kali Kardia €€ A fish restaurant on the harbourfront. The grilled octopus and the fresh fish platter are both highly recommended. 📍 Mastichari harbour 📞 22420 59289 🕒 Open 06.30–01.00

O Makis €€ Hidden in a back street just behind the harbour, a locals' restaurant noted for its *mezedes* and reasonably priced fresh fish. ⓐ Mastichari ☏ 22420 59061 🕒 Open 09.00–midnight, or later

Saloon Bar € Western-style snack bar and great cocktails. ⓐ Mastichari beach 🕒 Open 09.00–midnight; Happy hour 19.00–22.00

NIGHTLIFE

Nightlife in Marmari is pretty low key, with **Images** (ⓐ Main road ☏ 22420 41950 🕒 Open 19.00–05.00) and **No Name Bar** (ⓐ Opposite the Apollonia Hotel 🕒 Open 19.00–late) as current favourite haunts for cocktails. In Mastichari, there is a wider choice. The romantic, open-air **Acid Jazz Café** is popular after 21.00 (☏ 22420 59211 🕒 Open 19.00–late). At **Number One** there's Sky TV, showing sports and music from the 60s, 70s and 80s (☏ 69784 64439 🕒 Open 19.30–01.00, or later).

🔻 *The local fishing fleet brings a touch of colour to the harbour*

Kardamena
harbourfront action

Gently shelving white sands and an unruffled sea make Kardamena (pronounced 'Car-dam-ena') an ideal family resort, but the town really comes alive after the children have gone to bed. You can relax in one of the harbourfront restaurants, then tour the nightspots strung out along the edge of the bay where the entertainment ranges from big-screen TV to drinking challenges, dancing and karaoke.

Kardamena is the second-largest and fastest-growing package resort on Kos, and especially popular with Brits wanting a taste of home abroad. With its lively atmosphere, jam-packed beach and dazzling neon lights, it is hard to believe this former tiny fishing village was once known for its beauty and serenity. Today it remains just as beautiful, but it is now known for its continuous nightlife, attracting young people from all over Europe to its abundant bars, discos and clubs.

The resort's fantastic sand-and-shingle beach runs the length of the resort and is always packed by day. Water sports are popular, especially

⬇ *View towards the harbour front restaurants*

water-skiing, windsurfing and parasailing. And for those who prefer to stay on dry land, there's go-karting 3 km (2 miles) east of the resort. (☎ 22420 92065 ⏱ Open 11.00–23.00), sunbathing, and plenty of opportunities for walking and cycling.

Don't just party while in Kardamena! Be sure to take to the sea at least once. There are daily cruises to Nisyros island to visit the active **volcano** (page 88), day-trips to **Paradise Beach** (page 76), fishing trips or a half-day outings in small day-boats to the tiny island of **San Antonio** for keen swimmers and snorkellers.

THINGS TO SEE & DO
Antimachia Windmill ★★
The airport at Antimachia will already be familiar to visitors; but don't miss the nearby village with the only working windmill on the island.
⏱ Open 10.00–18.00

Cycling ★
On the main road near the taxi rank, **On Yer Bike** and **Bill** (☎ 22420 92273) have a selection of bikes, mopeds and quads for hire.

Kardamena Castle ★
High on a hill to the north of the village, you will see the ancient ruins of Kardamena Castle – a fabulous two-hour walk inland for the energetic, with a breathtaking panorama to reward your efforts. To find the start of the trail, walk eastwards from Starlight disco for 700 m (765 yds). Turn left at the crossroads and, after 500 m (550 yds), you will see a paved path on your right signed to the castle.

Plaka Forest ★★
Kos has more than 7200 hectares (17,800 acres) of forest. Picturesque Plaka, easily reachable by bike, is rich in wildlife, including hares, partridges and migratory birds. There are cool and refreshing spots for a picnic or a barbecue and several nature trails.

BEACHES

The Aqua Sports centres on **Kardamena beach** offer parasailing, water-skiing and windsurfing, etc. There are several swimming pools including Kool Pool, Harriet Pool and Blue Lagoon.

Buses run several times a day (from the taxi rank) to **Paradise Beach**, a beautiful expanse of white sand. At one end it is known as **Bubble Beach** because of the rising bubbles of gas, caused by volcanic activity.

RESTAURANTS

Aramis €€€ French and Greek food in a roof garden setting. Try one of the unusual sauces. Children's and vegetarian menus. ⓐ One street back from the waterfront ⓣ 22420 92056 ⓛ Open 18.00–23.00

Avli €€ Sit in the lovely garden and sample the best traditional Greek fare that Kardamena has to offer. ⓐ Main street ⓣ 22420 92100 ⓦ www.avlirestaurant.gr ⓛ Open 17.00–midnight

Chrisopoulos € A delightful blue-and-white taverna on the western edge of town, serving delicious home-made daily specials. ⓐ Kardamena beach ⓣ 22420 91235 ⓛ Open 09.00–23.00

Gianni's €€ Claims to be the oldest restaurant in Kardamena. Extensive menu; vegetarian choices. ⓐ Main street ⓣ 22420 91452 ⓛ Open 17.30–midnight

Posidonia €€ Greek food, right on the seafront with great views. Modestly priced ⓐ Seafront ⓣ 22420 91430 ⓛ Open 09.00–23.00

Scala Roof Garden €€€ Considered one of the best restaurants in Kardamena. Roof garden, sea view, delicious European cuisine. ⓐ Harbour ⓣ 22420 92444 ⓛ Open 08.00–midnight

Symposium €€ International menu ⓐ One street back from the waterfront ⓣ 22420 92068 ⓛ Open 17.00–midnight

NIGHTLIFE

Avantage Late-night bar with Greek music, more popular with locals than tourists. ⓐ Off the square ⓛ Open midnight–04.00 (06.00 at weekends)

Cheers Bar One of the main party bars. Live DJ with free tequila, vodka or schnapps with every drink ⓐ On the beachfront ⓛ Open 19.00–03.00

Crossroads Lively bar catering for football enthusiasts. The speciality is alcoholic jelly shots. ⓐ Bar Street ⓛ Open 10.00–03.00

Flamingos Carwash and party music make for a good atmosphere in this disco. ⓐ On the waterfront ⓛ Open 23.00–04.00 (06.00 at weekends)

Greg's Place Cocktail bar next door to Flamingos, with an attractive terrace shaded by vines. Popular with clubbers on their way home. The best place in town to see the sunrise! ⓐ Seafront ⓛ Open 10.00–07.00

Status Air-conditioned disco club with a large dance floor. House music. ⓐ Town centre ⓣ 22420 91645 ⓛ Open midnight–04.00 (until 06.00 at weekends)

SHOPPING

 The streets in Kardamena are unnamed but most shops are near the waterfront. **Louis supermarket** sells groceries and alcohol at reasonable prices, and the cream cakes and home-made ice cream at the bakery in the main square are delicious. **Flavours bakery** in the Square (ⓛ Open 24 hours) is a good source of midnight snacks. **Watermelon** and **Passadena** have clothes for all ages, while jewellery can be bought from **Gold Line** or **Enigma**.

Kefalos
the island's best beaches

The atmosphere of old Greece awaits you in the peaceful village of Kefalos, set on a hillside at the southernmost point of Kos, dominated by the imposing windmill of Papavasillis, and overlooking the spectacular long curve of Kamari Bay with its quiet beach and crystal-clear, shallow waters. Along the shoreline is Kefalos's newest beach resort – a long, thin development, with hotels spread along the beach road and a wide selection of traditional-style bars and tavernas.

In contrast to the busy resorts of Kos Town and Kardamena, Kefalos is gentle and relaxing, with some of the best beaches on the island. The main sand-and-shingle beach runs the entire length of **Kamari Bay** and overlooks a pretty island topped by the ancient church of **Aghios Nikolaos**. Here you will find plenty to occupy you, whether you fancy trying your hand at windsurfing, sailing, parascending or water-skiing, enjoying a fun trip on a pedalo, or simply lazing the hours away on a sun-lounger.

Should you tire of Kamari Bay, small boats shuttle visitors daily from Kefalos harbour to further sandy beaches just round the headland, with idyllic names such as **Paradise**, **Hawaii**, **Magic** and **Bubble Beach** (named for the volcanic gas vents in the tidal stream which turn the sea into an open-air jacuzzi). Alternatively, there are daily fishing trips, or excursions to **Nisyros** (page 88) and the **Turkish mainland** (page 82).

↘ During your stay in Kefalos, be sure to visit the neighbouring village and port of **Limionas**, renowned for its magical sunsets, its picturesque harbour and cove, and the island's best fish restaurant, the **Limionas Fish Taverna** (page 79).

RESTAURANTS

🍴 **Faros** €€ Alongside the fishing harbour, the 'Lighthouse' serves copious quantities of fresh fish as well as international dishes.
ⓐ Kefalos 📞 22420 71240 🕐 Open 09.00–23.00

◯ *Colourful boats in Kefalos harbour*

🍴 **The Great Aussie BBQ** €€ Cook your own choice of meat on the outdoor chargrill barbecue here. For a special gourmet treat, order yourself the surf 'n' turf platter (sirloin steak with prawns and lobster medallions in a cream sauce). ⓐ Main road, Kefalos ❶ 22420 71734 🕐 Open 08.00–23.00

🍴 **Limionas Fish Taverna** €€ Reputedly the best fish restaurant on Kos, and certainly one of the best places to view the setting sun. ⓐ Limionas harbour 🕐 Open 08.00–midnight

🍴 **Stamatia** €€ This traditional-style taverna, romantically situated on the beach, serves wholesome Greek cuisine. Try the *kleftiko* (lamb with mushrooms, garlic, mustard and wine) or *papousakia* (aubergine halves stuffed with minced meat and topped with a creamy white sauce). ⓐ Near Baywatch Watersports, Kefalos ❶ 22420 71245 🕐 Open 09.00–23.00

Taverna Katerina €€ Hidden down a bumpy track at Aghios Stefanos Beach (to the east of Kamari Bay), this delightful taverna serves fantastic fresh fish. Well worth the detour.
🅐 Kefalos ☎ 22420 71513 🕒 Open 08.00–22.00

Zefyros € A popular international restaurant, with a pretty flower-clad terrace overlooking the beach. Enjoy fresh fish, meat kebabs or spaghetti bolognese, all washed down with Greek wines.
🅐 Main road, Kefalos ☎ 22420 71873 🕒 Open 09.00–23.00

NIGHTLIFE

B52's The two most popular cocktails at this breezy waterfront bar are the 'Cactus' (the most alcoholic!) and 'Sex on the Beach'. 🅐 Kamari Bay road, Kefalos ☎ 22420 71395 🕒 Open 09.00–late (sunrise even!)

Opa-Opa This candlelit cocktail bar overlooking the beach is surely one of the island's most romantic haunts for an early evening drink. Later most evenings, there is a live DJ and dance music. 🅐 Main road, Kefalos ☎ 22420 71947 🕒 Open 09.00–02.00

Popeye's An English bar with a friendly atmosphere, draught beer, pool tables and Sky TV. There's also a disco at the back, with a live DJ playing Greek or dance music. 🅐 Main road, Kefalos ☎ 22420 71143 🕒 Open 17.00–03.30 (disco) ❶ Admission charge in season (free entry before midnight)

SHOPPING

Kefalos boasts a good selection of shops. **Tsoukalis** (🅐 On the main road) is one of the largest and best-stocked mini-markets in the resort. **Traditional** (🅐 Kamari Bay road, near the harbour) contains an excellent selection of sophisticated jewellery.

EXCURSIONS
Out & about

Marmaris
the Turkish experience

You will already have been tantalized by glimpses of the Turkish mainland from Greece – this is your chance to see it at first hand. The hydrofoil leaves from Rhodes harbour every day (except Sundays) at 08.30, and takes just 45 minutes to reach Marmaris, so there's plenty of time to take in the sights, do a bit of shopping and have a meal in a seafront *lokanta*.

Kaleiç is the diminutive, but picturesque old quarter of Marmaris. The castle dates from the 11th century but was enlarged by Suleyman the Magnificent in 1522 during his campaign to conquer Rhodes.

The **Bazaar**, a labyrinth of alleyways behind the promenade, is one of the liveliest on the Mediterranean coast. You can pick up some real bargains here, so long as you barter.

 Visitors require an exit stamp on their passports to visit Turkey, so it is best to book through an agent who knows the correct procedures.

THINGS TO SEE & DO
Atlantis Aquapark ★★
This attraction in Uzunyal is perfect for adults and children of all ages, with numerous convoluted water slides and rides. ◷ Open 10.00–18.00

SHOPPING
 Reliable shops within the Bazaar complex include:
Paradise Carpets For rugs and kilims. ❷ 42 Sokak 15
Goldium For jewellery. ❷ Yeni Çarsi Sokak 24
Gersu Leather For leatherware. ❷ Yeni Çarsi Sokak 24
Iris For perfumes and cosmetics. ❷ Tepe Mah 47
Don't forget to bargain. It is expected – even in shops.

Friday Market ★ ★ ★

Villagers converge on Marmaris once a week, clogging up the roads and
back streets with carts laden with produce. Definitely an experience not
to be missed.

BARS

Haç Mustafa Sokagi, universally known as 'Bar Street', is in the centre of
Marmaris. Here dancing continues until 05.00 at the height of the
season, but many bars are open during the day too.

◗ *Pop over to Turkey for a bit of shopping*

● *Explore Bodrum's blue bay*

Bodrum
top Turkish resort

Until a few years ago, Bodrum was a remote fishing village. Now, it is the undisputed tourist hotspot of the Turkish coast, a bustling, cosmopolitan resort with an unrivalled choice of shops and restaurants, yet it still retains the character of a traditional market town. It is also one of the prettiest towns on the Aegean coast, a mass of sugar-cube-shaped, whitewashed houses clustered around a dazzling blue bay. You can take a day trip from Kos harbour to Bodrum – the boat takes just an hour to get there.

Known in ancient times as Halicarnassus, Bodrum was the birthplace of Herodotus, the 'father of written history', and the site of the tomb of King Mausolus, one of the Seven Wonders of the World. Little remains today of ancient Bodrum apart from a few scattered ruins (including a well-preserved amphitheatre) and the spectacular medieval castle built by the Knights of St John, which guards the entrance to the harbour where elegant yachts crowd the palm-lined waterfront and the chic marina.

The reputation of Bodrum's boatyards dates back to ancient times and craftsmen can still be seen building traditional wooden boats, including the *gulet* (motor-yacht) with its distinctive broad beam and rounded stern, today mostly used for pleasure trips along the scenic Bodrum peninsula.

THINGS TO SEE & DO
Aquapark ★
Bodrum's first and Turkey's biggest water fun-park with 24 water slides, numerous restaurants and an action-packed programme of poolside entertainment. Be sure to try the Kamikaze slide, the Twin Twister and the Big Hole! ❸ Dedeman Aquapark, Ortakent/Yalikavak–Turgutreis junction (on Bodrum's western outskirts) ❶ (00 90) 252 358 5950 ❶ Open 10.30–18.30 ❶ Admission charge

SHOPPING

 Leatherware, cotton goods, jewellery, carpets, natural sponges and local blue-glass beads are among the best buys in the friendly little shops that line the narrow streets of Bodrum. The bustling **bazaar** (clothing, carpets and fabrics on Tuesdays; fruit and vegetables on Fridays) is full of excellent bargains, but you must haggle for a good price. Be careful when purchasing gold. It is priced by weight and the lowest carat is 14. Gold is not hallmarked in Turkey, so you need to get a certificate showing its weight and what carat it is. If the shop is not forthcoming with the necessary paperwork, think twice before buying.

Babil Center A sweet-smelling store containing Turkish Delight, herbs, spices, apple tea, honey, nuts and coffee. ➌ Kumbahçe Camii Alti (entrance in Uçkuyular Street)

Dalyanci Galeri The gaily coloured, handmade pottery here makes ideal gifts. ➌ Cumhuriyet Caddesi, Alim Bey Pasaji 55

There are also **Duty Free** shops in the harbour where you can purchase cigarettes and perfumes.

Bodrum Castle ★★

The medieval Castle of St Peter is a magnificent example of 15th-century Crusader architecture, built on the site of an ancient acropolis by the Knights of Rhodes. It has recently been converted into a stunning Museum of Underwater Archaeology, with treasures salvaged from shipwrecks dating back to the Bronze Age. ● Open Tues–Sun 08.30–noon and 13.00–17.00 ❶ Admission charge

Turkish Bath ★

Treat yourself to an authentic Turkish Bath at the recently opened Bodrum Hammam. There are separate sections for men and women and massages (oil or scrub) are also available. ➌ Cevat Sakir Caddesi, Fabrika Sokak ❶ (00 90) 252 313 4129 ● Open 06.00–midnight

You will usually get a better deal if you pay for goods in sterling (although you will need Turkish lire for food and drink). If you purchase goods by credit card, you may lose any discount given.

RESTAURANTS

Epsilon €€ An atmospheric restaurant specialising in both international and Turkish dishes, including a wide variety of tasty *mezedes*. ⓐ Türkkuyusu Mah Keles Çikmazi ⓣ (00 90) 252 313 2964 ⓛ Open 11.00–midnight

Lokanta € The Turkish equivalent of a *tapas* bar. No need to worry if you don't speak Turkish because all the dishes are on display and all you have to do is point at what you want. ⓐ Cumhuriyet Caddesi 115 ⓣ (00 90) 252 316 8383 ⓛ Open 11.00–midnight

Nur €€ This typical old Bodrum house with its bougainvillaea-clad courtyard is the perfect choice for a romantic meal. The menu contains a good choice of classic Turkish and international dishes. ⓐ Cumhuriyet Caddesi ⓣ (00 90) 252 313 1065 ⓛ Open noon–23.00

● *Bodrum offers an unrivalled choice of shops and restaurants*

EXCURSIONS

Nisyros
volcanic island

This seductive island was formed millions of years ago by volcanic activity and the giant crater, Stephanos, is still the main attraction for visitors. You'll also see olives, figs, lemons and almonds all growing in abundance on the terraced slopes above Mandraki, the island's tiny port where life has changed little in the last 2000 years. Excursion boats run regularly between Kos harbour and Nisyros, taking around an hour to get there.

The volcano has been intermittently active for centuries, and although the last major eruption was in 1888, continuous seismic activity has now been recorded for more than two years. The largest of five craters, Stephanos measures an astonishing 300 m (328 yds) across. You'll need strong shoes for the 22 m (72 ft) descent which, incidentally, is made at your own risk. There is an overpowering stench of sulphur dioxide (think rotten eggs) but it's a price worth paying for this once-in-a-life-time opportunity.

THINGS TO SEE & DO
Mandraki ★★
Mandraki, which is the main port of Nisyros, is a delightful town of whitewashed houses. Its narrow alleys are overlooked by two ruined castles and one of several religious centres on the island – **Spilliani Monastery** (🕐 Open 10.30–16.00), with its striking solid gold altar. If you think the 120 steps up to the monastery are hard work, spare a thought for the womenfolk of Mandraki who, on 25 August each year, climb them on their knees as a gesture of reverence! The bird's-eye view from the top makes the climb worthwhile.

Pali ★★
Just 4 km (2½ miles) from Mandraki, this picturesque fishing port is popular with visitors for its sandy beaches and wonderful tavernas.

RESTAURANTS

Aphrodite €€ Reputedly the best taverna in Pali, known for its fresh fish and meat dishes, served with Rhodian wine straight from the barrel. ⓐ Waterfront, Pali ⓣ 22420 31242 ⓛ Open 07.00–midnight

Hellinis Taverna € This friendly waterfront taverna serves highly recommended Greek, international and fresh fish dishes. ⓐ Waterfront, Pali ⓛ Open 08.00–23.00

Mike's Taverna €€ At the heart of Mandraki, Mike's Taverna specialises in traditional Greek cuisine, including such vegetarian dishes as *maghirefta* (vegetable casserole) and *pitia* (a typical Nisyros dish made with chickpeas). ⓐ Waterfront, Mandraki ⓣ 22420 31378 ⓛ Open 08.00–midnight

Tony's Taverna € This Australian-owned taverna is ideal for a light lunch by the water's edge. ⓐ Waterfront, Mandraki ⓣ 22420 31509 ⓛ Open 08.00–midnight

SHOPPING

Shopping on Nisyros is always a pleasure. In Mandraki, look out for **Artin Caracasian**'s photographic studio (ⓐ On the left-hand side of the main street as you head uphill from the port), where you can purchase magnificent photographs of the island, and the **Sunflower craft shop** (ⓐ On the right-hand side of the main street as you head uphill from the port), which sells delightful pottery, glass and jewellery, some of which uses obsidian, a precious black glass-like stone from neighbouring Yali island that was once used by Hippocrates for his cutting instruments.

Some of the food stores sell the island's delicious speciality, *soumadha* (a milky almond drink), and the tiny village **bakery** in Pali sells crusty brown bread – a rarity in Greece.

Kalymnos
island of the sponge divers

The fourth-largest island in the Dodecanese, Kalymnos (Kalimnos) is famous for the sponges that are sold from the quayside warehouses of Pothia, the busy main port. Here visitors can learn about the colourful history and traditions of the industry and see how the sponges are cleaned and treated. Ferries leave Mastichari three times a day for Pothia.

Apart from Pothia, the island's other attractions include thermal springs, caverns dripping with stalactites, crumbling Byzantine ruins and numerous coves and beaches, perfect for swimming and sunbathing.

In times gone by, sponge fishermen dived naked and unprotected (sometimes to depths of 75 m/246 ft), weighted with heavy stones and carrying a rope as a lifeline. Today's fishermen wear regulation wetsuits and carry oxygen tanks, but diving remains a hazardous business. Sadly, disease has wreaked havoc among the Mediterranean sponges and the industry has fallen sharply into decline – only a couple of boats now put regularly to sea.

The people of Kalymnos still mark the annual departure of the fishermen, usually just after Orthodox Easter, with an exuberant festival called *Iprogros* (Sponge Week).

 Kalymnos always seems to be a degree or two hotter than Kos, so be sure to wear a sun-hat, use a high-factor protective suncream and drink plenty of water.

SHOPPING
Apart from the stalls selling shells and sponges, try **Kalypso** (❷ In an alley beside Anastasio bar) for jewellery and pottery, the **Bottle Store** (❷ On the waterfront) for local wines, and **To Petrino** in Enoria Christou (❷ Just off the waterfront) for unusual gift ideas.

THINGS TO SEE & DO
Nautical and Folklore Museum ★★
This small but fascinating museum vividly recounts the remarkable history of the island and its heroic sponge divers. ❸ Beside the cathedral ◷ Open 08.30–14.30 ❶ Admission charge

Pothia ★★★
Behind the many harbour-front cafés and tavernas of Pothia, the island's capital, lies hidden an original Greek town, totally unspoilt by tourism, with its tiers of multi-coloured houses lining the narrow streets and stepped alleyways. It is said that the houses are pastel-washed according to the residents' status or profession – blue for fishermen, pink for newly-weds, and so on. It also boasts one of the four cathedrals of the Dodecanese islands (along with Rhodes, Kos and Karpathos), countless churches and several splendid Venetian-style municipal buildings, which adorn the seafront.

Pserimos ★★
Many excursion boats leaving Kalymnos for Kos stop off for a couple of hours at Pserimos, enabling people to swim in the crystal-clear waters and to enjoy the sandy beach of this idyllic little island.

RESTAURANTS & BARS
Anastasio € This shady café-bar on the waterfront is a popular stop for a cool drink. ❸ On the waterfront ◷ Open 08.00–15.00 and 18.00–01.00

Omilos €€ You will be made welcome at this hospitable restaurant, which serves a variety of local specialities. ❸ Beside the docks ◷ Open 07.00–15.30 and 18.00–midnight

Symposium € A trendy snack bar, next door to Anastasio, which attracts a young crowd. They also sell the most divine, locally produced ice cream. ❸ On the waterfront ◷ Open 09.30–midnight

Symi
monasteries and mansions

Cameras click furiously as the excursion boats round the headland into Yialos, the main port of the spectacularly beautiful island of Symi. Rising above the harbour are tiers of elegant, neo-classical mansions, coloured predominantly ochre with blue, green or orange shutters. It takes approximately an hour and a half to get here by boat from Mandraki harbour.

THINGS TO SEE & DO
Panormitis ★★

The delightful little harbour is dominated by the monastery of St Michael the Archangel and its gaily painted bell tower. The church, illuminated only by the gleam of lamps and incense burners, contains the resplendent armour-clad figure of St Michael. The monastic museum contains miniature ships, wax dolls, icons by Fabergé, and a beautifully fashioned mother-of-pearl crib, as well as an assortment of rural and domestic bric-à-brac. Pilgrims sometimes stay in the monastery overnight, occupying the numbered rooms off the main courtyard.

Yialos ★★★

A flight of 375 steps lead from the harbour to the old town of **Chorio**, a maze of winding alleys and typical village houses. There are wonderful views, and the church contains a mosaic floor depicting a mermaid enticing seamen to their doom. Look out for the 19th-century pharmacy, complete with apothecary jars, and the folklore museum housed in an elegant mansion, with a reconstructed interior of a traditional Symiot house (🕓 Open Tues–Sun 10.00–14.00 ❶ Admission charge). If you follow the signs up to Kastro, you will find an acropolis, knights' castle and traces of prehistoric walls.

◀ *Yialos is a spectacularly beautiful port*

BEACHES
Local taxis will take you to the tiny fishing hamlet of **Pedi**, the nearest sandy beach, and boat-taxis run to **Nimborio** or to the more secluded beaches on the eastern coast, including **Aghia Marina** and **Aghios Georgios**.

RESTAURANTS & BARS

Mouragio €€ Fish is the speciality at this typical waterfront restaurant, but omelettes, pizzas, salads, spaghetti, *souvlaki* and grilled chicken are also available if you prefer. ❸ On the harbourfront (heading towards the tiny beach) ◕ Open 08.00–16.00 and 19.00–23.00

Neraida €€ A popular restaurant in the main square, offering traditional Greek dishes, home-made pasta and good wines. ❸ Main square ❶ 22460 71841 ◕ Open 11.00–15.30 and 19.00–midnight

Thelos € Magnificent harbour views. Menu includes Greek, international and daily-changing fish dishes. ❸ On the waterfront (beyond the Harani boatyard) ◕ Open 11.00–15.00 and 19.00–23.00

Vapori € Friendly bar in Yialos harbour, with an excellent choice of snacks, drinks and cocktails. ❸ At the start of the 375 steps up to Chorio ❶ 22460 72082 ◕ Open 08.00–01.00

SHOPPING
Buy painted icons in the **monastery shop** at Panormitis and sponges from the **Aegean Sponge Centre** in Yialos. **Harbour stalls** sell honey, olives, oils and boxes of herbs and spices.

Food & drink

LOCAL FOOD

Greek cooking uses the freshest ingredients and is nourishing, tasty
and filling. As very little produce is imported, dishes are based on local
foodstuffs. Vegetarians, however, will find their options fairly limited
because even vegetable dishes may be cooked with beef stock. So,
although in every resort you will be sure to come across English and
international standards, be sure not to miss out on the delicious food
that the islands have to offer.

APPETISERS

A typical Greek meal begins with a basket of fresh bread and a selection
of *mezedes* (appetisers). Order several dishes and share them with
your friends. The highlights are *horiatiki*, a refreshing salad comprising
feta cheese, tomato, cucumber and black olives; *tzatziki* (cucumber
yoghurt dip); *taramossaláta* (a paste of cod roe and lemon juice) and
saganaki (fried cheese fritter). Cheese or spinach pies also make good
snacks – try *kopanisti*, a soft, tasty cheese (usually feta, which is made
with goat's milk) with red-hot peppers.

MAIN COURSES

Meat is cheap and plentiful. The most succulent dishes include *souvláki*
or *shish kebab* – garlic-marinated lamb dressed with onions; *keftedes*
– meatballs with mint, onion, eggs and bacon; moussaka – layers of
minced lamb with sliced aubergine and bechamel sauce; *kleftiko* –
slow-cooked lamb; and *stifado* – beef with onions and tomato sauce.
Or you might like to try *dolmades* – vine-leaf parcels stuffed with rice,
minced lamb and pine kernels and braised in lemon and olive oil.

Fishermen's catches of red mullet, sole, snapper or sea bream may
be brought to your table if you've found a good seaside taverna.
Before ordering, remember that fish is sold by weight; establish the
price first – a good rule of thumb is that one kilo serves four people.

Prawns, stuffed mussels, fried squid and stewed octopus (often

● *Be sure not to miss out on authentic Greek food*

cooked in white wine, with potatoes and tomatoes) are all widely available. Swordfish steaks are also popular, served grilled with lemon, salt and pepper.

If you suddenly become peckish around lunchtime but don't want to sit down to a full meal, *gyros* – doner kebab in pitta bread – or the snack version of *souvláki* – pitta bread filled with meat, tomato and onion – will fill a hole.

DESSERTS
Most Greeks will settle for fresh fruit after a meal – the watermelons are unbelievably juicy – or there are apricots, peaches and grapes. If you have a sweet tooth, try *baklava*, a pastry soaked in honey with almonds and walnuts, *loukoumades*, a kind of honey fritter, or *bougatsa*, a hot pie with a creamy filling of custard and cinnamon. More revitalising on a hot day is yoghurt topped with honey and almonds – delicious!

DRINKS
Soft drinks, like colas and lemonades, are sold everywhere but freshly made orange or lemon juice is more refreshing in hot weather. Mineral water (still or fizzy) is equally thirst-quenching – Greek brands are perfectly safe and acceptable. Outside the hotels, tea generally means hot water and a teabag because Greeks don't generally drink it as we do.

Greek coffee is served in small cups, is strong in flavour, has a treacly texture and leaves a thick sediment. Ask for *gliko* if you like it sweet, *metrio* (medium), or *sketo* (without sugar). If you prefer you can order espresso or instant (ask for Nes). In resorts, cappucino is increasingly available. And there's nothing more refreshing on a hot day than a *frappé* (iced coffee).

WINE & BEER
The most distinctive Greek wine is *retsina*. Flavoured with pine resin, it takes some getting used to and you may prefer it with lemonade or soda water. *Retsina* is supposed to complement the oil in Greek food, though it is definitely an acquired taste. The best local wines are produced by the Emery and the CAIR companies of Rhodes. Emery's Villaré, a prize-winning dry white, is reputed to be one of the best in Greece. CAIR's offerings also include a light, red table wine, Chevalier de Rhodes. Equally good value are the sparkling wines, Grand-Prix and Brut.

Greek lager is very drinkable and cheaper than imported beer – ask for Mythos or Hellas. The most widely available foreign brands are Heineken, Amstel, Kronenberg and Budweiser. Specify that you want bottled or draught beer, as cans are often a great deal more expensive.

SPIRITS

The Greek national drink is *ouzo*, an aniseed-flavoured spirit usually drunk as an aperitif. *Ouzo* can be consumed straight, but if you intend to have more than one glass, follow custom and dilute it with water. You may also be offered *raki*, a spirit made from distilled wine, grape skins and pips. Greek brandy is also highly palatable, and available in various strengths and prices, indicated by star ratings (3, 5, 7). The best-known brand, Metaxa, is dark and sweet, but you could also ask for the drier Kamba.

🔺 *A typical Greek salad makes a great starter*

LIFESTYLE

Menu decoder

Here are some of the authentically Greek dishes that you might
encounter in tavernas or pastry shops.

dolmadákia Vine leaves stuffed with rice, onions, dill, parsley, mint and
lemon juice

domátes/piperiés yemistés Tomatoes/peppers stuffed with herb-
flavoured rice (and sometimes minced lamb or beef)

fassólia saláta White beans (haricot, butter beans) dressed with olive
oil, lemon juice, parsley, onions, olives and tomato

lazánia sto fourno Greek lasagne, similar to Italian lasagne, but often
including additional ingredients, such as chopped boiled egg or sliced
Greek-style sausages

makaronópita A pie made from macaroni blended with beaten eggs,
cheese and milk, baked in puff pastry

melitzanópita A pie made from baked liquidized aubergines mixed with
onions, garlic, breadcrumbs, eggs, mint and parmesan cheese

melitzanossaláta Aubergine dip made from baked aubergines,
liquidized with tomatoes, onions and lemon juice

moussakás Moussaka, made from fried slices of aubergines,
interlayered with minced beef and *béchamel* sauce

píta me kymá Meat pie made from minced lamb and eggs, flavoured
with onions and cinnamon and baked in filo pastry

pastítsio Layers of macaroni, haloumi cheese and minced meat
(cooked with onions, tomatoes and basil), topped with *béchamel*
sauce and baked

saláta horiátiki Country salad (known in England as 'Greek salad'); every
restaurant has its own recipe, but the basic ingredients are tomatoes,
cucumber, onions, green peppers, black olives, oregano and feta
cheese dressed with vinegar, olive oil and oregano

souvláki Kebab – usually of pork cooked over charcoal

spanakotyropitákia Cigar-shaped pies made from feta cheese, eggs,
spinach, onions and nutmeg in filo pastry

taramossaláta Cod's roe dip made from puréed potatoes, smoked cod's roe, oil, lemon juice and onion

tyropitákia Small triangular cheese pies made from feta cheese and eggs in filo pastry

tzatzíki Grated cucumber and garlic in a dressing of yoghurt, olive oil and vinegar

⬇ *Stuffed vine leaves are a local speciality*

THE KAFENEION

In Greek villages, the *kafeneion* (café) remains very much a male preserve, although visitors of both sexes will be made welcome. Customers come here to read the paper, debate the issues of the day and play backgammon, as well as to consume *café hellenico* (Greek coffee). This is made by boiling finely ground beans in a special pot with a long handle. Sugar is added during the preparation rather than at the table, so you should order *glyko* (sweet), *metrio* (medium) or *sketo* (no sugar). In summer, try *frappé* (with ice).

Shopping

Rhodes clearly has more shopping opportunities than Kos, owing to its size. On both islands, the vast majority of shops are found in the main towns.

LOCAL SPECIALITIES

Certain villages have their own specialities and you'll find it cheaper to buy on the spot. On Rhodes, Lindos, for example, is famous for pottery, while the stallholders of Siana can't wait to sell you jars of locally produced honey. You can buy wines and liqueurs at wholesale prices from the **Emery Factory** in Embonas or, if it's natural sponges you're after, the divers on Kalymnos will be sure to oblige.

If you see something you like but aren't happy about the price, try polite negotiation; alternatively, walk away with a disappointed look on your face – there's a good chance the trader will call you back.

JEWELLERY

Gold (usually 18 carat) and silver are priced by weight and can be exceptional value because there's such a small mark-up for the workmanship. Most distinctive is the jewellery inspired by ancient Greek or Byzantine designs.

LEATHER GOODS

The choice includes shoes, thonged sandals, bags, satchels, purses, wallets, belts (check stitching and buckles before leaving the shop). For something more unusual, visit Archangelos on Rhodes to order a pair of distinctive made-to-measure peasant boots which protect against snakes!

HANDICRAFTS & LOCAL PRODUCE

Look out for brightly coloured *kourelia* (rag rugs), ceramics (for example hand-painted vases, plates, cockerels, mock fruit and other novelties), painted glass, gift-wrapped baskets of herbs, oils, hand-painted

● *Greece is a good place to find brightly-coloured ceramics*

wooden icons, embroidered linen table-cloths and Greek Delight, along with other gooey sweets.

Little blue and white evil eyes will keep you and your family safe. Onyx chess sets, alabaster classical statuettes and silver theatre masks are popular souvenirs, as are *brikis* which are small metal containers used for boiling Greek coffee – you can buy packets of the coffee in local stores.

Kids

For families with young children, Faliraki (Rhodes) and Kardamena (Kos) are the best beaches. Both are gently shelving, with acres of soft sand and handy shops where you can stock up on snacks, soft drinks, ice creams, inflatables, and so on. Beaches on the western coasts are great for waves but watch out for strong currents – young children should stay within the roped-off areas or swim in the hotel pools.

PLAYGROUNDS

Many resorts have small playgrounds with swings, slides, see-saws and climbing frames (unsupervised). Luna Park mini-car tracks at Kremasti and Trianta on Rhodes are suitable for children up to the age of 12 and offer a choice of buggies and motor bikes – all equipped with seat belts.

Children won't complain about the uphill walk to the Acropolis at Lindos if you let the donkey take the strain. The price of the donkey ride often includes a souvenir photograph.

BOATING ADVENTURES

Snorkelling excursions are especially suited to energetic children who are also good swimmers. There's the thrill of diving from the deck of a boat into crystal-clear water, then swimming with the fish and exploring the rocky shoreline. Some snorkelling equipment is provided. See your holiday rep for details. These trips are not advisable for very young children.

VOLCANO

Journey to the island of Nisyros (page 88) to see a real live volcano – a once-in-a-lifetime experience and a good talking point for the children when they return to school. Watch the steam rise from the crater and feel the sticky surface underfoot.

◀ *Keep the kids entertained at a water park*

⬤ *Why not hire a bike to explore the island?*

Sports & activities

ON THE ISLAND OF RHODES

Golf Afandou, is the island's only 18-hole (par 73) championship golf course and was designed by British golf architect, David Harridine. It is open 12 months a year and has a clubhouse, bar, changing rooms.
📞 22410 51256

Mini-golf can be enjoyed in many of the large resorts. There are excellent courses at the **Olympic Palace Hotel** in Ixia (📞 22410 39790 🕐 Open 10.00–midnight) and the **Cannon Bar**, Faliraki (📞 22410 85596 🕐 Open 08.00–midnight).

Hiking One of the best walks is to the top of Profitis Ilias Mountain (altitude 720 m/2360 ft). The ascent takes around three hours. There's a great café at the summit serving mountain tea and fresh yoghurt and honey. Walking tours can be arranged with local guides. For full information, contact the tourist office or your holiday rep, or get a good map and go it alone.

Sailing Rhodes is the busiest centre in the Aegean for yachting. A variety of craft – bare-boat or crewed, sail or power – are available from the **Yacht Agency Rhodes** (❶ 22410 22927). The usual minimum hire period is three days, but day excursions are possible. Catamaran sailing is possible from Faliraki beach.

Snorkelling At Kalithea Spa – a small bay and lido 4 km (2½ miles) south of Rhodes, built in the 1920s. Excellent swimming, snorkelling and scuba diving. Hippocrates drank – and recommended – the healing properties of the spa waters here. Today the domed pavilions stand abandoned and the waters have long since dried up.

Turkish baths The Sultan's *Hamman*. A great place to steam away holiday excess. Selections for men and women. Take your own towels and soap. ❸ Archelaou/Ippodamou Streets (Old Town). ❶ Open to the public Tues–Sat 07.00–19.00

Windsurfing Conditions on Rhodes, especially in the west of the island, are among the best in the world. For more information, contact **Blue Horizon** ❸ On Ialyssos beach ❶ Open 09.00–19.00 ❶ 22410 95819

ON THE ISLAND OF KOS
Water sports, including pedalos, water-skis and sailboards, are available from stands on the beach in many island resorts. There is also a large choice of sporting activities available on Kos – most are based at hotels.
- **Aquapark** ❸ Psalidi, Kos Town ❶ 22420 30125
- **Ideal Bikes** ❸ Eth. Antistasis, Kos Town ❶ 22420 29003
- **Kos Yachting Club** ❸ Lambi ❶ 22420 20055
- **Marmari Horse Riding Centre** ❶ 6944 104446 (mobile)
- **Tennis** ❸ Continental Palace, Kos Town ❶ 22420 22737
- **Tennis and mini-golf** ❸ Achileas Beach, Mastichari ❶ 22420 59161
- **Water sports** ❸ Caravia, Marmari ❶ 22420 41291
- **Water sports and tennis** ❸ Akti, Kardamena ❶ 22420 92777

Festivals & events

DANCE

To dance the Greek way, you need to be in touch with the spirit of the music – what the Greeks call *kefi* (soul). Summer festivals and village weddings are the best places to see local variations like the *mekhanikos*, the Kalymnos sponge fishers' lament. ⓦ www.nostos.com/dance has more information about specific dances

The **Nelly Dhimoglou school** holds classes in traditional and modern Greek folk dancing (ⓐ Open-air theatre, Old Town, Rhodes, behind the public baths ❶ 22410 20157 ⓛ Sept–May). The same company gives performances in an attractive garden setting (ⓐ The Old Town Theatre, Andronikou Street, Rhodes Town ⓛ June–Oct Mon, Wed and Fri at 21.20).

MUSIC

Visitors are likely to encounter traditional folk music played on the *bouzouki*, a pear-shaped, stringed instrument plucked like a mandolin. You can hear traditional Greek music most nights at **Resalto** and **Cashmir** in the Old Town. ⓦ www.greeka.com/greece-music.htm provides a brief survey of traditional Greek music.

FESTIVALS

Most Greek festivals are religious in origin. Apart from big celebrations like Easter, you're most likely to see *panegyria*, local festivals celebrating the patron saint of the village church or monastery with music and dancing. On 24 June, bonfires are lit all over Kos Island to celebrate the **feast of St John the Baptist**. On 26 July, **St Panteleimon** is honoured in Siana (Rhodes) with drinking, dancing and a service of thanksgiving in the church. Similar celebrations take place on Kalymnos. The **Hippocratia festival**, held in Kos in August, features art exhibitions, concerts, theatre performances and films, culminating in a re-enactment of the swearing of the Hippocratic Oath in the Asklepion. The **Feast of the Assumption**, from 15 to 23 August, sees one of the largest and most boisterous celebrations in the Dodecanese taking place in Kremasti (Rhodes).

Preparing to go

GETTING THERE

The cheapest way to get to Rhodes or Kos is to book a package holiday with one of the leading tour operators specializing in Greek island holidays. Most of the larger islands have airports, but if you choose to visit one of the smaller ones, it may be a case of taking a plane and then a boat.

If your travelling times are flexible, and if you can avoid the school holidays, you can also find some very cheap last-minute deals using the websites for the leading holiday companies.

BEFORE YOU LEAVE

Holidays should be about fun and relaxation, so avoid last-minute panics and stress by making your preparations well in advance.

It is not necessary to have inoculations to travel in Europe, but you should make sure you and your family are up to date with the basics, such as tetanus. It is a good idea to pack a small first-aid kit to carry with you containing plasters, antiseptic cream, travel sickness pills, insect repellent and/or bite relief cream, antihistamine tablets, upset stomach remedies and painkillers. Sun lotion can be more expensive in Rhodes and Kos than in the UK so it is worth taking a good selection especially of the higher protection factor lotions if you have children with you, and don't forget to take after-sun cream as well. If you are taking prescription medicines, ensure that you have enough for the duration of your visit – you may find it impossible to obtain the same medicines in Rhodes and Kos. It is also worth having a dental check-up before you go.

DOCUMENTS

The most important documents you will need are your tickets and your passport. Check well in advance that your passport is up to date and has at least three months left to run (six months is even better). All children, including newborn babies, need their own passport now, unless they are already included on the passport of the person they are travelling with. Remember it generally takes at least three weeks to process a passport renewal and that this turnaround time can be longer in the run-up to the summer months. For the latest information on how to renew your passport and the processing times contact the Passport Agency ☏ 0870 521 0410 (24 hours) ⓦ www.ukpa.gov.uk

You should check the details of your travel tickets well before your departure, ensuring that the timings and dates are correct.

If you are thinking of hiring a car while you are away, you will need to have your UK driving licence with you. If you want more than one driver for the car, the other drivers must have their licence too.

🔺 The islands' roads are not usually busy

MONEY

There are cash machines that can be used with Switch and credit Cards at main airports and in major towns. If you are going to a small resort, check the facilities first. You can exchange money at the airport before you depart. You should also make sure that your credit, charge and debit cards are up to date – you do not want them to expire mid holiday – and that your credit limit is sufficient to allow you to make those holiday purchases. Don't forget, too, to check your PIN numbers in case you haven't used them for a while – you may want to draw money from cash dispensers while you are away. Ring your bank or card company for help.

INSURANCE

Have you got sufficient cover for your holiday? Check that your policy covers you adequately for loss of possessions and valuables, for activities you might want to try – such as scuba-diving, horse riding, or water sports – and for emergency medical and dental treatment, including flights home if required.

After January 2006, a new EHIC card replaces the E111 form to allow UK visitors access to reduced-cost, and sometimes free state-provided medical treatment in the EEA. For further information, ring EHIC enquiries line ☎ 0845 605 0707, or visit the Department of Health website Ⓦ www.dh.gov.uk

CLIMATE

Rhodians enjoy a typical Mediterranean climate: hot, dry summers and cool, wet winters. From May to September you will hardly see a day of rain. July and August are rather hot – it is best to stay out of the sun from 11.00 to 15.00, especially older people and very young children. Use a sun-block at all times, especially on fair skin. A sunhat and sunglasses are essential. Drink lots of water, and try not to drink alcohol while sunbathing.

The climate in Kos is good from May to November, but in April it can get a little wet and windy, and the same applies from September onwards. A light jacket or cardigan is a must for early evenings at the beginning and end of the season.

SECURITY

Take sensible precautions to prevent your house being burgled while you are away:

- Cancel milk, newspapers and other regular deliveries so that post and milk does not pile up on the doorstep, indicating that you are away.
- Let the postman know where to leave parcels and bulky mail that will not go through your letterbox – ideally with a next-door neighbour.
- If possible, arrange for a friend or neighbour to visit regularly, closing and opening curtains in the evening and morning, and switching lights on and off to give the impression that the house is being lived in.
- Consider buying electrical timing devices that will switch lights and radios on and off, again to give the impression that there is someone in the house.
- Let Neighbourhood Watch representatives know that you will be away so that they can keep an eye on your home.
- If you have a burglar alarm, make sure that it is serviced and working properly and is switched on when you leave (you may find that your insurance policy requires this). Ensure that a neighbour is able to gain access to the alarm to turn it off if it is set off accidentally.
- If you are leaving cars unattended, put them in a garage, if possible, and leave a key with a neighbour in case the alarm goes off.

AIRPORT PARKING & ACCOMMODATION

If you intend to leave your car in an airport car park while you are away, or stay the night at an airport hotel before or after your flight, you should book well ahead to take advantage of discounts or cheap off-airport parking. Airport accommodation gets booked up several weeks in advance, especially during the height of the holiday season. Check

TELEPHONING RHODES & KOS

To call Rhodes or Kos from the UK, dial 00 30 followed by the nine-digit number.

whether the hotel offers free parking for the duration of the holiday – often the savings made on parking costs can significantly reduce the accommodation price.

PACKING TIPS

Baggage allowances vary according to the airline, destination and the class of travel, but 20 kg (44 lb) per person is the norm for luggage that is carried in the hold (it usually tells you what the weight limit is on your ticket). You are also allowed one item of cabin baggage weighing no more than 5 kg (11 lb), and measuring 46 by 30 by 23 cm (18 by 12 by 9 inches). In addition, you can usually carry your duty-free purchases, umbrella, handbag, coat, camera, etc, as hand baggage. Large items – surfboards, golf-clubs, collapsible wheelchairs and pushchairs – are usually charged as extras and it is a good idea to let the airline know in advance that you want to bring these.

CHECK-IN, PASSPORT CONTROL AND CUSTOMS

First-time travellers can often find airport security intimidating, but it is all very easy really.

- Check-in desks usually open two or three hours before the flight is due to depart. Arrive early for the best choice of seats.
- Look for your flight number on the TV monitors in the check-in area, and find the relevant check-in desk. Your tickets will be checked and your luggage taken. Take your boarding card and go to the departure gate. Here your hand luggage will be X-rayed and your passport checked.
- In the departure area, you can shop and relax, but keep an eye on the monitors that tell you when to board – usually about 30 minutes before take-off.
- Go to the departure gate shown on the monitor and follow the instructions given to you by the airline staff on when to board the plane.

During your stay

AIRPORTS

Rhodes has now expanded its airport and you will find a small stand for spirits and last-minute souvenirs, a kiosk with magazines, newspapers and snacks on the ground floor, a café on the second floor, and a large sitting area in case of delay. Customs are based there, and anyone flying in from non-EU countries will be subject to a customs check.

When you arrive in Kos there may be short delays at the airport when collecting your luggage, but transfers only take 15–35 minutes depending on the area you are going to. At the airport there are snack bars and a duty free area.

BEACHES

In summer, many beaches have life guards and a flag safety system. Make sure that you are familiar with the flag system for Rhodes and Kos. Other beaches may be safe for swimming but there are unlikely to be lifeguards or life-saving amenities available. Bear in mind that the strong

○ Make sure you know the beach flag warning system

winds that develop in the hotter months can quickly change a safe beach into a not-so-safe one, and some can have strong currents the further out that you go. If in doubt, ask your local representative or at your hotel.

TOURIST INFORMATION

For information on the islands themselves try:

National Tourist Organisation of Greece ⓐ Corner of Makeriou and Papagou Streets, Rhodes ⓣ 22410 23655 ⓦ www.gnto.gr ⓛ Open Mon–Fri 08.30–14.00

For the latest on what's happening in Rhodes Town and Kos Town, call in at one of the tourist information offices:

City of Rodos Information Office ⓐ Rimini Square, Mandraki ⓣ 22410 35945 ⓛ Open Mon–Fri 08.00–21.00, Sat 08.00–15.00, closed Sun

Kos Municipal Tourist Information ⓐ Atki Kondourioti ⓣ 22420 24460/26595 ⓛ Open Mon–Fri 08.00–22.00, Sat 08.00–15.00

Also see the latest edition of *Rodos News* or Kos Life, published in English and available free of charge from tourist information offices and hotels, and the invaluable island guide *Where and How in Kos*, available at most tourist shops.

CHILDREN'S ACTIVITIES

There are lots of opportunities for both daytime and evening fun: go-karting, water parks, a unique ostrich farm, Rodini Park, Luna Parks, cinemas, and an indoor play-park at Planet Z. You could also visit the Strike bowling alley café, and the aquarium, or go horse riding or cycling. Kids particularly enjoy seeing the island while riding on the miniature trains in Rhodes Town and Faliraki.

Around the city of Kos and the villages you will always find a playground, and an aqua park with many attractions for children of all ages. Most large hotels have special facilities for children and also trained staff to entertain them.

> **BEACH SAFETY**
> Most beaches where the public bathe in numbers operate a flag
> system to indicate the sea conditions.
> * **Red (or black)** = dangerous – no swimming
> * **Yellow** = good swimmers only – apply caution
> * **Green (or white)** = safe bathing conditions for all

CONSULATES
There is a British Vice-Consulate on Rhodes and Kos and an Irish
Consulate on Rhodes.
British Vice-Consulate Rhodes ⓐ 29 Gr. Lambraki Street, Rhodes ❶ 22410
22005 ⓦ www.britishembasssy.gov.uk ❶ Open Mon-Fri 09.00–14.00
British Vice-Consulate Kos ⓐ 8 Annetas Laoumtzi, Ag. Marina, Kos
85300, above the offices of Aelos Travel ❶ 22420 21549
Irish Consulate ⓐ 111 Amerikis Street, Rhodes ❶ 22410 75655 ❶ Open
Mon–Fri 09.00–14.00

If any advice is required or if you have problems with the police or have
an accident, it's best to first contact your tour representative if possible,
and then the Vice-Consulate. Both consulates offer emergency numbers
for out of hours.

CURRENCY
The currency in Greece is the euro and it is possible to change your
sterling for euro at most hotels' reception desks, banks or any of the
exchange offices that are dotted around the towns. Look for the word
trapeza. Always remember to take your passport with you when you
change money. The most convenient way to obtain euros is by using
an ATM (Automated Teller Machine). There are ATMs outside banks
in most resorts. The small villages do not generally have exchange
services, so if you go out for a day ensure you have enough money to see
you through the day. Euro (€) note denominations are 500, 200, 100, 50,

20, 10 and 5. Coins are 1 and 2 euros, and 1, 2, 5, 10, 20 and 50 céntimos.
If you are going to Turkey, you will need Turkish lira.

Banks ◷ Open Mon–Thurs 08.00–14.00, Fri 08.00–13.30, closed Sat, Sun
and holidays. A few branches in Rhodes Town and Lindos open Sat
09.00–13.00

Credit cards These are widely accepted at resort hotels, luxury shops and
larger restaurants.

DRESS CODES

Casual attire is acceptable everywhere, but try to dress conservatively
when visiting archaeological sites, museums, churches or monasteries.
It is not appropriate to show bare arms and legs.

While vacationing during the summer months, bring lightweight,
casual clothing and good walking shoes. During May, June, September and
October the weather is warm during the day but you will need a light
jacket in the evening as the tropical breeze takes over.

ELECTRICITY

Rhodes and Kos have 220V electrical outlets. You will need an adaptor
plug for any electrical equipment you bring with you and these can be
purchased at the local supermarkets or in the UK before you depart.
At times in high season there may be power-cuts lasting at most
two hours, but usually much less.

 If you are considering buying electrical appliances to take home,
always check that they will work in the UK before you buy.

FACILITIES FOR THE DISABLED

Over the past few years there have been many ramps built onto beaches,
hotel and restaurant entrances, to help tourists visiting in wheelchairs. You
may experience some difficulty while visiting archeological sites, so it is
best to travel with assistance. The Old Town in Rhodes has cobblestones
and long hills that can be tiring for those who are less able.

Some hotels in Kos have facilities for disabled people, but there are very few taxis or even buses that can cope with a motorised wheelchair. Some of the local buses do have disabled access, but this is normally restricted to people on foot, not in wheelchairs. There are many bars and restaurants that are on the level or have ramps. These are mainly in the city of Kos, but some can be found in Kardamena, Kefalos and Tingaki as well.

GETTING AROUND

Car hire and driving: parking fees (meters), have just been introduced in Rhodes Town, so be careful not to get a ticket when parking your rental car! The fees are levied Mon–Fri 09.00–14.30 and 17.00–21.00, Sat 09.00–14.00. Sun/Bank Holidays are free.

The rules for parking are:

- Blue lines – parking with ticket
- Yellow lines – official services only (pharmacies, embassies etc)
- White lines – free parking

The meters are numerous and usually no more than a block away in any direction. They take Euro coins – retrieve the ticket from the machine and place it on the dashboard of your car.

Always make sure you have your driving licence as you cannot hire a car, motorbike or moped without one. Helmets must be worn on motorbikes by law. If you break down, contact the number on the vehicle key and they will assist you.

Public transport Travelling with the locals by bus could be a pleasant and less expensive experience. There are bus schedules posted down by Mandraki Harbour on Rhodes for all island destinations.

Taxis Usually located in main squares, although you should be prepared to wait in line during high season and rush hours. **Radio Taxi** in Rhodes (🌐 22410 64712) is a well-established taxi service that the hotel or restaurant/venue can call – charges are standard throughout the island and taxis have meters inside. Expect them to add a surcharge after midnight. Please note that they come rather quickly so be prepared to leave within minutes of phoning, as they may not wait around as long as you might expect.

HEALTH MATTERS

Health hazards: it is not necessary to have special injections for travelling to Greece. Care should be taken in the sun, and if you are on medication, your health practitioner should be consulted before you leave the UK as to what effects, if any, the climate could have on your medication.

Private medical clinics are now available throughout the island offering a more personalised and, in most instances, quicker response to medical needs. The staff is multi-lingual. All doctors speak English and can make house/hotel calls. A variety of insurances is accepted. Each facility has a number of doctors and health workers, and can usually perform minor surgery if necessary.

Clinics in Rhodes These are situated in Faliraki, Pefkos, Kalithea, Ixia, and Rhodes Town. ☎ 22410 30020 (Rhodes Town)
Clinics in Kos Dr Kaliopi Hatzinikolaou ☎ 22420 92111 (Kardamena)
Dr Sebastian Papachristos ☎ 22420 29639 (Kos Town)
Water The water in Greece has a high mineral content so it may be best to drink bottled water during your stay. The water served in hotels, bars, restaurants, tavernas is quite safe to drink.

WHAT TO DO IN AN EMERGENCY
If your rep is not available to help, then the following phone numbers may be useful, although not everyone will speak English:

Police and ambulance ☎ 100
Fire ☎ 199
Hospitals (Rhodes Town) ☎ 22410 80000
Hospitals (Kos) ☎ 22420 22300
Tourist police (Rhodes) ☎ 22410 27423
Tourist police (Kos) ☎ 22420 26666
Lost and found (Rhodes) ☎ 22410 23294

THE LANGUAGE

The beauty of Greek is that it is phonetic. Greeks love to hear visitors attempt to speak it. However, most signs are in Greek and English, and English is so widely – and well – spoken that you can happily trundle through a fortnight without needing a word of Greek.

The Greek alphabet

Greek	Name	Pronunciation	Greek	Name	Pronunciation
A α	alpha	a (as in apple)	N ν	ni	n as in no
B β	beta	v (as in vase)	Ξ ξ	xi	x/ks as in xerox
Γ γ	gamma	g/y, becomes y in front of e and i	O o	omicron	o as in opera
Δ δ	delta	th as in the	Π π	pi	p as in pope
E ε	epsilon	e as in extra	P ρ	rho	r as in roll
Z ζ	zeta	z as in zest	Σ σ	sigma	s as in safe
H η	eta	i/e as in eat	T τ	taf	t as in table
Θ θ	theta	th as in theme	Υ υ	ypsilon	e as in these
I ι	iota	i/e as in these	Φ φ	fi	f as in fire
K κ	kappa	k/c as in keep	X χ	hi	kh as in Bach
Λ λ	lamda	l as in limit	Ψ ψ	psi	ps as in corpse
M μ	mi	m as in mother	Ω ω	omega	o as in opera

ENGLISH

General vocabulary

GREEK (pronunciation)

ENGLISH	GREEK (pronunciation)
yes/no	*neh/ Okhee*
please/thank you	*parakahLO/ efkhareesTO*
hello/goodbye	*YAsoo/ andEEo*
good morning	*kahleeMEHRa*
good afternoon/evening	*kahleeSPEHRa*
good night	*kahleeNEEKHtah*
excuse me/sorry	*signomEE*
Help!	*VoyIthia!*
today/tomorrow	*siMEHRa/ AHvrio*
OK	*enDACKsee*

ENGLISH	**GREEK** (pronunciation)
Useful words and phrases	
yesterday	*ekTES*
open/closed	*anikTON/ klisTON*
right/left	*thexiA/ aristerA*
How much is it?	*POso kAni?*
Where is a bank/post office?	*Poo Ine i TRApeza?/to tahithromEEo?*
Where is the bus station?	*Poo Ine o stathMOS ton iperastiKON leoforEEon?*
stamp	*grammatOseemo*
doctor/hospital	*YAHtros/nosokoMEEo*
police	*assteenoMEEa*
I would like...	*Tha Ithela...*
menu	*menOO*
toilets	*tooahLEHtess*
mineral water	*emfialoMENo nerO*
bread	*psomEE*
salt/ pepper	*alAHti/ pipEri*
fish/meat	*psarEE/ krEas*
beer/wine	*bEEra/ krasEE*
Cheers!	*Steen eeyEEa soo!/YAHmas!*
coffee with milk	*kafEs (me gAla)*
Can we have the bill, please?	*Mas fErnete ton logariasmO, parakalO?*
I don't understand	*then katalaVENo*
Do you speak English?	*MilAteAnglikA?*

MEDIA

The city's official website ⓦ www.rhodes.gr, has a wealth of historical information and an interactive map showing places of interest. The main newspapers written in Greek are the *Rodiaki* and *Prodos*, The local TV channel for Rhodes is Channel 4. Most hotels with televisions do offer satellite TV. 102 Radio International reports the news in five different languages. Between 10.00 and 11.00 you can listen to world news in English.

> **TELEPHONING ABROAD**
> To call the UK from Rhodes or Kos, dial 00 44 followed by the area code (minus the initial 0) and then the number you require.

The electronic edition of Greece's English language newspaper is a good source of national and international news (W www.ekathimerini.com). There's also a section detailing festivals around Greece. English newspapers are available in most tourist resorts, although they are mostly a day late. Radio and television are usually in Greek, but the hotels often have satellite TV and European programmes can be found.

OPENING HOURS
Banks on Rhodes are normally open Mon–Thurs 08.00–14.00, Fri 08.00–13.30, Shops open Mon–Fri 09.00–14.00 and 17.00–08.30. Sat 09.00–14.00. Breakfast ends around 10.00, lunch is usually between 13.30–15.30 and dinner starts late – 20.00 hours is on the early side.
    Banks on Kos are open Mon–Thurs 08.00–14.00 and Fri 08.00–13.30. Tourist shops are open daily from 08.30 till late, but ordinary shops operate from 09.00–13.00 and 17.00–20.30 Mon–Fri, and morning hours only on Sat.

PERSONAL COMFORT AND SECURITY
The crime rate is low in Rhodes and Kos, but you should take certain precautions that you would when travelling anywhere in the world, eg lock your valuables in a hotel safe. Be alert when retrieving money from an ATM. Don't try to purchase narcotics or bring them into the country.

RELIGION
The religion here is Greek Orthodox and there are many churches around the islands. It is possible to enter some of them, but please be respectful and cover up before you go in. There is also a Catholic church in Kos Town and services are held on Sunday only at 10.00.

TELEPHONES

The cheapest way is to purchase a telephone card from a supermarket and use the telephones dotted around the streets. Kronocarta is the new international calling card, which can be used from the privacy of your hotel phone rather than using a phone box. There is a minimal calling charge for an outside line, and the cards can be purchased from all newspaper kiosks.

TIME DIFFERENCES

Greece is two hours ahead of the UK. Time changes in both spring and autumn coincide with the rest of Europe.

TIPPING

Tipping is up to the individual but a tip of 5–10 per cent of the bill in a restaurant, taverna or bar is about right. Taxi drivers don't expect tips but if you are happy with the service, give a tip.

WEIGHTS AND MEASURES

The metric system is used in Greece.

Imperial to metric	Metric to imperial
1 inch = 2.54 centimetres	1 centimetre = 0.4 inches
1 foot = 30 centimetres	1 metre = 3 feet, 3 inches
1 mile = 1.6 kilometres	1 kilometre = 0.6 miles
1 ounce = 28 grams	1 gram = 0.04 ounces
1 pound = 454 grams	1 kilogram = 2.2 pounds
1 pint = 0.6 litres	1 litre = 1.8 pints
1 gallon = 4.6 litres	

INDEX

ACKNOWLEDGEMENTS

We would like to thank all the photographers, picture libraries and organizations for the loan of the photographs reproduced in this book, to whom copyright in the photograph belongs:
B and E Anderson (pages 1, 5, 8, 15, 115);
Teresa Fisher (page 27, 56, 57, 58, 64, 70, 72, 79, 95, 111);
Ivy Press (page 101);
Jupiter Images Corporation (pages 108, 125);
Pictures Colour Library Ltd (pages 92, 104);
Thomas Cook Tour Operations Ltd (pages 11, 13, 22, 24, 28, 32, 38, 40, 44, 48, 51, 69, 74, 81, 83, 84, 87, 99, 103, 106).

We would also like to thank the following for their contribution to this series:
John Woodcock (map and symbols artwork);
Becky Alexander, Patricia Baker, Sophie Bevan, Judith Chamberlain-Webber, Stephanie Evans, Nicky Gyopari, Krystyna Mayer, Robin Pridy (editorial support);
Christine Engert, Suzie Johanson, Richard Lloyd, Richard Peters, Alistair Plumb, Jane Prior, Barbara Theisen, Ginny Zeal, Barbara Zuñiga (design support).

Send your thoughts to
books@thomascook.com

- **Found a beach bar, peaceful stretch of sand or must-see sight that we don't feature?**
- **Like to tip us off about any information that needs a little updating?**
- **Want to tell us what you love about this handy, little guidebook and more importantly how we can make it even handier?**

Then here's your chance to tell all! Send us ideas, discoveries and recommendations today and then look out for your valuable input in the next edition of this title. And, as an extra 'thank you' from Thomas Cook Publishing, you'll be automatically entered into our exciting monthly prize draw.

Send an email to the above address or write to:
HotSpots Project Editor, Thomas Cook Publishing, PO Box 227, Unit 15/16, Coningsby Road, Peterborough PE3 8SB, UK.